# THE
# VEGETARIAN
## HANDBOOK

*Also by Rodger Doyle*
THE COMPLETE FOOD HANDBOOK (with James L. Redding)

# THE
# VEGETARIAN
# HANDBOOK

A Guide to
Vegetarian Nutrition and Foods

## RODGER DOYLE

CROWN PUBLISHERS, INC., NEW YORK

*T O*
## Doris

Printed in the United States of America
Published simultaneously in Canada by
General Publishing Company Limited

Designed and illustrated by Ruth Kolbert Smerechniak

**Library of Congress Cataloging in Publication Data**
Doyle, Rodger P
The vegetarian handbook.

1. Vegetarianism.  2. Vegetarian cookery.
I. Title.
TX392.D68      613.2'6      78-11744
ISBN 0-517-53470-3
ISBN 0-517-53471-1 pbk.

Second Printing, October, 1979

# CONTENTS

Preface
vii
A Note on Terminology
x

PART TWO

## VEGETARIAN FOODS AND RECIPES

## APPENDIXES

# PREFACE

Vegetarians are like left-handed people in a right-handed world. Most of the nutritional advice they see on TV or in periodicals is planned with meat eaters in mind. There are dozens of reliable textbooks on nutrition but none of them has a section on vegetarianism. The most authoritative American text, *Modern Nutrition in Health and Disease*, is over 1100 pages long and weighs five and a half pounds, but it contains only five passing references to the problems of vegetarians.

Vegetarians need a reliable, concise source of information on nutrition and foods. They should have easy access to the facts about the special dietary problems they will face in pregnancy, infancy, and adolescence. They should be able to find out about the requirements of vegetarian athletes. They should have reliable information about the different types of vegetarian diets, such as the vegan (no animal food) and the fruitarian. Are they safe? Are they practical? Are they worthwhile? They should be able to find out quickly and easily about vegetarian foods. Which are the most valuable? Where are the best places to buy them? What are the best ways to cook them? (Or should you eat them raw?) They should have information on ways for vegetarians to lose weight. They should know about the pitfalls of vegetarian diets.

Reliable information on vegetarian diets is available but it's scattered in scores of articles in medical journals, government publications, and in books on food science. Some of the information is unpublished and is known to only a few physicians who have had practical experience in handling vegetarian problems.

Part I of this book brings together all of the facts from these sources likely to be of practical use to vegetarians and would-be vegetarians. It contains many suggestions on vegetarian nutrition and foods, including menu recommendations. In every case these recommendations are in line with the dietary allowances set by the National Academy of Sciences and the National Research Council. In Part I, I have emphasized the importance of variety. Nutritionists don't know all of the nutrients required by the human body. By eating a wide variety of foods, you reduce the risk that some as yet undiscovered nutrient is missing from your diet. Vegetarians by definition choose from fewer food groups than omnivores and so it is even more important for them to choose from among the widest possible number of foods compatible with their principles.

I want to emphasize that the nutritional recommendations in Part I apply to normally healthy people and are not intended as therapy for disease. Those with disease should consult their physician before adopting any of the suggestions in this book. Another point that merits emphasis is the importance of keeping your physician informed of your diet. This applies particularly to those on a vegan (no animal food) diet during the critical periods of growth, pregnancy, and lactation.

Advice on nutrition wouldn't be complete without practical information on foods and how to prepare them. In Part II you'll find a discussion of vegetarian foods including possible pitfalls associated with some of them. The recipes in Part II are those that I've found to be most useful for good nutrition and good eating.

No book on nutrition would be very interesting (or useful) if it didn't discuss many of the newer though often highly tentative ideas that appear in the medical journals. New hypotheses are constantly being proposed, tested, and challenged. I have referred to many of these less than fully tested ideas in this book. In these cases, their tentative nature is indicated by such words or phrases as "association," "suggested cause," or "possible cause." In some cases I refer to studies of laboratory animals. Conclusions from such studies cannot, of course, be applied with complete confidence to humans.

A lay person with the temerity to write about nutritional matters must obviously have guidance from professionals in the field. I am most fortunate in having had the advice of Loretta Spotila (M.S. Nutrition), who examined in detail the manuscript of Part I and suggested many improvements. My conversations with F. R. Ellis, M.D., FRCPath., and T. A. B. Sanders (Ph.D. Nutrition) were extremely useful in helping me to shape the sections on vegan nutrition. I am also greatly indebted to both Dr. Ellis and Dr. Sanders for taking the time from their busy schedules to comment on extensive portions of the manuscript. I am deeply indebted to Dr. U. D. Register, chairman of the Department of Nutrition, Loma Linda University School of Health, for his kindness in suggesting improvements in several passages dealing with protein and cholesterol. My thanks also to Dr. B. J. Meyer of the Department of Physiology, University of Pretoria, for commenting on the section dealing with fruitarian diet; and to Dr. David Pendergast of the Department of Physiology, State University of New York at Buffalo and Dr. David L. Costill, Director, Human Performance Laboratory, Ball State University, for clarifying certain points regarding the role of carbohydrates in sports nutrition. Nancy B. Chrisman, executive director of the Dairy Council of the Niagara Frontier has been most helpful in supplying information and clarifying points relating to the nutritive value of dairy products.

I wish to thank James L. Redding, who, by challenging many of the statements in the first draft, helped to sharpen my thinking on a number of points. Broady Richardson's comments on the early chapters were most useful in improving the concept of the book.

I am grateful to H. Lee Freshhood, Ph.D., and Mrs. Sara Cummings, consulting nutritionist, both of the Tennessee Department of Public Health, and particularly to J. O. Williams, M.D., of Mt. Pleasant, Tennessee, and to Margaret Nofziger for their patience in clarifying the nutritional program at The Farm in Summertown, Tennessee. I also wish to thank K. W. Heaton, M.D., FRCP, University of Bristol; Bruce Armstrong, M.D., University of Western Australia; Edward H. Kass, M.D., Harvard Medical School; and Roland Phillips, M.D., Loma Linda University School of Health, for clarifying certain points in their published studies.

My thanks go to the many prominent leaders of the vegetarian movement in America and Great Britain who provided valuable insights into the background of the movement. In particular, I thank Dr. Gordon Latto, president of the International Vegetarian Union; H. J. Dinshah, president of the North American Vegetarian Society; and Mrs. Kathleen Jannaway, secretary of the British Vegan Society.

I am grateful to Dr. Irma B. Vyhmeister, to her co-authors at Loma Linda University, and to the W. B. Saunders Company for permission to use material from their article in Volume 24 of *Pediatric Clinics of North America*; to the American Alliance for

Health for permission to use material from *Nutrition For Athletes*; to the National Academy of Sciences for permission to reproduce material from *Recommended Dietary Allowances*, Eighth Edition; to the World Health Organization and Dr. R. Passmore for permission to reproduce material from the *Handbook of Human Nutritional Requirements*; and to the Department of Health and Welfare for permission to reproduce material from *Dietary Standard for Canada*.

I wish to thank Mrs. Lorraine Corcoran for typing the many drafts and the final manuscript of this book, and also Fred Derf, who checked many of the figures. My thanks also to C. K. Huang, director of The Health Science Library, State University of New York at Buffalo, and the many members of the library staff who, by their thoughtfulness and courtesy, greatly facilitated my research.

# A  NOTE  ON  TERMINOLOGY

This book deals mainly with two types of vegetarians: *lacto-vegetarians* and *vegans*. Labeling these groups is often a problem and a source of confusion. The term *lacto-ovo vegetarian*, sometimes used to describe those who eat dairy products and eggs, as well as fruits and vegetables, has the virtue of precision, but it's just too awkward. Instead, I've used the term *lacto-vegetarian* or simply *vegetarian*. Often, I'll use the word *vegetarian* to cover both lacto-vegetarian and vegan, but this will be apparent in context.

Those who eliminate not only meat but also dairy products and eggs have been called by various names, including *pure vegetarian*, *strict vegetarian*, and *vegan*. I've yet to meet anyone who calls himself a pure vegetarian or a strict vegetarian, but since there are many who call themselves vegans, I use this term here.

At times I also refer to *omnivores*, *fruitarians*, and *macrobiotics*. An omnivore, as the term is generally used, eats any flesh food—beef, pork, veal, lamb, poultry, or seafood—in addition to dairy products and plant foods. Fruitarians, sometimes also called raw food eaters, eat only raw fruit, vegetables, nuts, and sprouted seeds and grains. Macrobiotics practice a variety of diets, including the omnivore, lacto-vegetarian, and vegan.

PART ONE

# VEGETARIAN NUTRITION

# 1

# A Strategy
# for Vegetarian Nutrition

Before World War II most medical researchers believed that the major killers of our time—heart disease, stroke, and cancer—were largely the unavoidable consequences of aging. Today, forty years later, there is a feeling of optimism that these diseases are not inevitable. The optimism arises from the widespread recognition that the environment, including the food we eat, plays a major role in their development.

The evidence for the role of diet began to accumulate more than sixty years ago. During World War I, when the Allied blockade cut off most imports into Denmark, the Danes were faced with an alarming food shortage. For years they had depended on foreign sources for more than half their bread grains and for much of their animal foods. In this extreme situation, the Danish government in 1917 turned to Dr. Mikkel Hindehede of the Laboratory for Nutrition Research in Copenhagen. His advice: stretch available grain supplies by slaughtering the livestock and using the grain as human food. And so, for more than a year, most Danes became virtual vegetarians, with their principal fare being barley, porridge, potatoes, green vegetables, milk, and a limited amount of butter. Their staple bread was whole-grain rye with wheat bran added, a high-fiber food.

Many Danes lost weight, perhaps, as Dr. Hindehede suggested, because they didn't find their new diet palatable. However, the general improvement in their health was startling: during the food emergency, the death rate from noninfectious diseases fell by 34 percent.

Norway had a similar experience under the Nazi occupation in World War II. The Norwegians had less meat, whole milk, cheese, cream, eggs, fruit, and sugar, but ate more fish, skimmed milk, cereals, potatoes, and vegetables. They ate fewer calories, including less fat, less sugar, and less cholesterol, and their consumption of fiber went up. During the war, deaths from strokes, heart disease, and other cardiovascular diseases fell by 21 percent.

The Danish and Norwegian experiences are not isolated phenomena but follow a pattern found in many other countries under the privations of wartime. In Sweden, Finland, and England, which had food rationing during World War II, there was a decline in the death rate from cardiovascular disease, but after the war, when rationing was lifted, the rates shot up.

Medical researchers are cautious about drawing firm conclusions from these wartime experiences,* but they suspect that diet played a major role in reducing disease. But what specific dietary changes might have been beneficial? A simple reduction in calories? In fat? In cholesterol? In refined sugar? In meat? An

---

* Comparison of disease rates over time can be invalidated by changes in diagnostic practices and classification procedures. However, the widespread similarity of the statistical patterns among several countries makes it reasonable to assume that wartime conditions did indeed have a beneficial effect on health. Nondietary influences such as the wartime shortages of tobacco and increased physical activity due to fuel shortages could have had an influence on disease rates. The declines in tobacco usage may not be important. More men than women smoke, yet in the Norwegian experience during World War II, both sexes enjoyed proportionately equal declines in circulatory diseases. It is not clear to what extent changes in physical activity were an influence on disease. By modern American standards, pre–World War II Europeans were highly active people.

increase in consumption of fiber? Of vegetables? Some combination of these?

Surprisingly, almost sixty years after Hindehede's original report, there is less than complete agreement among medical researchers on specific dietary measures for preventing disease. Every nutritionist knows that many of us eat too much and that it is desirable to maintain normal weight. Beyond this there is controversy and the controversy is particularly heated over the role of fiber, sugar, fat, and cholesterol. Let us examine these controversies and see what bearing they have on nutrition for vegetarians.

## FIBER AND DISEASE

Will a high-fiber diet help to prevent disease? A group of highly respected British physicians, including Dennis Burkitt and Hugh Trowell, believe that it does. According to their theory, a high-fiber diet, by cutting bowel transit times, allows less time for bacteria to convert bile salts into potential carcinogens. Rural Ugandans, who hardly ever get cancer of the colon, eat considerable fiber. Americans and Europeans, who are much more apt to suffer from the disease, generally get far less fiber. There's some skepticism among medical researchers about this theory because not all the facts agree with it. Among Westerners, there is no evidence of a relationship between length of bowel transit time and the incidence of colon cancer. Country by country, cancer of the colon seems to follow more closely the consumption of fat rather than fiber. This, of course, does not eliminate the possibility that fiber may play a role in the disease.

According to Burkitt, Trowell, and certain other British physicians, a high-fiber diet may also protect against a variety of other diseases, including heart disease, appendicitis, gallstones, deep-vein thrombosis, hemorrhoids, diabetes, and diverticulosis. High-fiber diets are now used in the treatment of diverticulosis, a disease in which little pouches form in the alimentary tract, particularly the colon. Except for the successful treatment of this disease and the treatment of constipation, there is no firm evidence of the value of fiber. There is no evidence that fiber *prevents* diverticulosis or any other condition except constipation.

A substantial amount of fiber in the diet may eventually prove to be important for health. Vegetarians should not be concerned with lack of it. One study showed that lacto-vegetarians got 50 percent more than meat eaters, while vegans—those who don't eat animal food—got 50 percent more than lacto-vegetarians.

## SUGAR AND DISEASE

Sugar has become the nutritional villain of our age, but except for its role in causing dental caries, the case against it isn't all that solid. John Yudkin, the well-known British nutritionist, believes that sugar contributes to heart disease, but the evidence suggests that there is a much closer relationship between heart disease and fat. Recent work with young monkeys shows that excessive sugar may promote high blood cholesterol and possibly high blood pressure levels but it's not clear, at least yet, whether sugar has this effect on young children. There is a long-term project under way by a team from the Louisianian State School of Medicine in which thousands of children are being studied to determine which factors influence blood cholesterol and blood pressure levels. A report won't be available until sometime in the 1980s.

For years, some scientists have attempted to link excessive sugar consumption with diabetes. The evidence that it causes the disease isn't conclusive but it may act indirectly by contributing to obesity. Obese people are more apt to get diabetes, but it's not clear that obesity is actually to blame. Some researchers have speculated that diabetes may lead to obesity rather than the other way around.

There is a plausible but not fully confirmed case for sugar as a cause of obesity. Unprocessed foods, including sugar-rich fruits, are digested and absorbed slowly and so there is time for the body's normal hunger-depressing mechanisms to work. Refined sugar is so much more rapidly digested and absorbed that the normal mechanisms may go awry. According to another hypothesis, refined sugar may, through an intricate metabolic process, actually lead to greater accumulation of body fat than the same amount of calories from less refined foods. Nutritional scientists don't agree on the causes of obesity but universally recommend drastic reduction in sugar in treating the condition.

The most recent bad news about sugar comes from tests of rats made by Yudkin and his colleagues in England. According to their study, rats who were allowed to eat as much sugar as they wished suffered kidney damage, while those who were given starch instead had normal kidneys.

On the average, Americans and Britons consume about 4½ ounces of refined sugar a day or the equivalent of over 500 calories. Most nutritionists believe that this is too much even for healthy people of normal weight, not only because it promotes dental caries, but also because it displaces more nutritious foods and in some cases leads to deficiencies of some important nutrients. If you follow one of the suggested food plans in Chapter 2, you will be getting adequate nutrients. A good rule to follow, if you have the willpower, is to avoid candy and sugary desserts altogether, and to use sugar sparingly, only as a flavoring agent to make nutritious foods more palatable.

Sugar *is* a nutritional villain, but in the opinion of a large number of nutritionists (perhaps most) dietary fat is the archvillain.

## FAT AND CARDIOVASCULAR DISEASE

The three major risk factors in coronary heart disease and other cardiovascular ailments are considered to be high blood cholesterol, high blood pressure (hypertension), and smoking. High blood cholesterol is believed to contribute to atherosclerosis, the degenerative process of the arteries that underlies cardiovascular diseases. Consumption of saturated fat raises blood cholesterol while polyunsaturated fat lowers it.

Cholesterol doesn't travel loose in the blood but is carried around in packets composed mainly of fat and protein. These packets, called *lipoproteins*, are suspended in the blood much as droplets of oil are suspended in Italian salad dressing. Two of these substances, the *high-density lipoproteins* (HDLs) and the *low-density lipoproteins* (LDLs) are now considered by many researchers to be particularly important as indicators of heart attack risk and the risk of other cardiovascular diseases.

Recently, there has been impressive evidence that the amount of HDLs in the blood is inversely related to the probability of having a heart attack. According to one study, HDLs block the uptake of LDLs into the cells of the arterial wall. In other words, they appear to interfere with the basic process of atherosclerosis. The level of HDLs is partly determined by inheritance and tends

to be high among those who don't smoke, who exercise vigorously, and who are under standard weight. According to
some researchers, those who quit smoking, exercise considerably more, and lose weight raise their level of HDLs. There is
some tentative evidence that restriction of fat and substitution of
polyunsaturated for saturated fat may also raise levels. Women
have higher levels than men, a fact which may partly explain
their lower rate of heart attacks. Some researchers suspect that by
raising the level of HDLs the risk of cardiovascular disease is
reduced, but this theory has not yet been adequately tested.

LDLs are also considered to be predictors of heart disease: the
higher the level, the greater the statistical risk of heart attack. The
amount of LDLs in the blood is raised by eating saturated fat.
Experiments with animals have shown that when they are fed
too much food rich in saturated fat, their LDLs rise, they develop
atherosclerosis, and they suffer heart attacks, strokes, or lose
their limbs due to poor circulation. Many researchers, including
Dr. William Castelli, director of laboratories for the well-known
Framingham Heart Study, feel that the same process goes on in
humans. There is considerable epidemiological evidence sup-
porting this view. In the United States, the Netherlands, and
Finland, for example, the incidence of coronary heart disease is
about ten times that in Japan and Greece. Characteristically, the
Americans, Dutch, and Finns eat large amounts of saturated
fat—over 15 percent of their calories is in this form—while the
Japanese and Greeks take less than 10 percent of their calories as
saturated fat.

The American Heart Association has taken the lead in per-
suading the public that proper diet is extremely important in
preventing cardiovascular disease. The Association recommends that everyone now on a typical American diet eat less fat,
less saturated fat, and more polyunsaturated fat in order to lower
blood cholesterol levels. Not everyone endorses the Heart Association's approach. Many medical researchers agree with Dr.
Edward Ahrens, a specialist in the chemistry of lipids (fatty
substances) at Rockefeller University, who believes that recommendations like those of the AHA are simplistic and raise false
hopes. Like most others, he recognizes the statistical relationship between a high level of LDLs and cardiovascular disease but
believes that it is "not yet clear" that lowering the level in the
blood reduces the danger. Dr. Ahrens, like other critics of the
AHA, sees no *harm* in eating less fat and feels that it might even

be beneficial for a few. His principal objection to such diet plans is the implied promise that they will protect most of us against heart attacks and strokes. Instead, he recommends a more selective approach in which those who seem to be at risk are given special treatment.

If analysis of your blood indicates a risk, your physician will undoubtedly recommend special measures, including curtailing of dietary fat and cholesterol. But if you are healthy, is it worthwhile to restrict fat? In the opinion of many medical researchers, eating less fat is a wise move, for it may reduce not only the risk of cardiovascular disease, but also the risk of certain types of cancer.

## FAT AND CANCER

Dr. Ernest L. Wynder, president of the American Health Foundation, suggests that as many as 50 percent of cancers among women and one-third among men are related to nutrition. Among other preventative measures, he places strong emphasis upon eating less fat. Many cancer specialists agree with Dr. Wynder and believe that a reduction of dietary fat may lessen the chances of getting leukemia and cancer of the colon, rectum, breast, and possibly also cancer of the ovaries, uterus, testicles, and prostate. Some of these, such as cancer of the colon, are widespread in the United States and in other places where people eat a high-fat diet, but not in India, Japan, and most of Africa and Latin America, areas where much less fat is eaten.

Studies of laboratory animals give some support to the theory that fat may be a cause of certain types of cancer. When rats are fed high-fat diets, they develop cancer of the colon and breast. No one is certain why this happens, but there is a suspicion that it may do so by creating metabolic imbalances that promote the production of carcinogens. According to the theory advanced by some researchers, cancer of the colon occurs when fat in the intestines creates an environment in which certain types of carcinogen-producing bacteria thrive. One researcher suggests that a high-fat diet promotes breast cancer by upsetting the ratio of certain hormones in the body. Others have attempted to link excessive amounts of polyunsaturated fat to breast cancer.

## HOW MUCH FAT SHOULD YOU EAT?

The average American or Briton gets 40 percent or more of his calories from fat, a level that many researchers consider far too high. Several governments, including those of the Scandinavian countries, the USSR, and Italy, take the position that fat should be restricted to well below the 40 percent level. Other governments, including those of the United States and Great Britain, have adopted no official stand.

In this book, I've taken the position that it's wise for those with typical American or British fat consumption levels to cut back. A moderate reduction in fat from typical levels is unlikely to do harm. On the other hand, as we've seen, excessive dietary fat is a possible risk factor in cardiovascular disease and several types of cancer. Furthermore, fat can be a potent contributor to obesity: ounce for ounce, it has two and a quarter times as many calories as either protein or carbohydrates.

Many vegetarians have no problem in keeping their fat consumption well below the average of 40 percent. Other vegetarians, particularly those who eat substantial amounts of dairy products, can easily consume sizeable amounts of fat.* Gourmet vegetarian dishes, which have lately become popular, usually contain large amounts.

How much fat is too much? Several professional and official organizations have laid down guidelines that apply to average, normally healthy individuals:

*Recommended Percent of Calories from Fat*

| | |
|---|---|
| American Heart Association | maximum of 35% |
| British Cardiac Society | maximum of 35% |
| Medical Boards of Finland, Norway, and Sweden (joint recommendation) | 25 to 30% |
| USSR | maximum of 30% for males, 35% for females |
| Italy | maximum of 25% for adults, 30% for children and adolescents. |

* A person who eats two ounces of cheddar cheese, two cups of milk, six pats of butter, one cup of ice cream, one egg, two tablespoons of salad oil, and two ounces of peanuts in a day will get about 1200 calories in fat. For an average man eating the Recommended Dietary Allowance of 2700 calories, this amount of fat

Some experts, such as Drs. William and Sonja Connor of the University of Iowa College of Medicine, recommend an even lower level for adults—20 to 25 percent.

Is it possible that the official organizations have set the maximum amount of fat too high? Scientists are naturally cautious about recommending a more radical reduction, particularly when the evidence linking disease and diet is incomplete. This is not true of the Longevity Foundation of America, a group of non-nutritionists that has received much publicity. The Foundation recommends a maximum of 10 percent fat. It is not clear whether such drastic restriction has any health advantage over the less severe restriction recommended by the AHA and other organizations. In Japan, the traditional rice-based diet supplies only 10 percent of calories as fat. Some experts believe that this low fat consumption, and particularly the extremely sparse amount of saturates, explains the low incidence of coronary heart disease among the Japanese. Other experts disagree. A low-fat diet should theoretically have no adverse consequences for healthy adults if protein, vitamins, minerals, and essential fatty acids are supplied in adequate quantities.

The AHA recommends that you get less than 10 percent of calories from saturates and up to 10 percent from polyunsaturates. (The balance of fat calories would come from monounsaturates, which have no effect on blood cholesterol.) The Connors recommend not more than 5 to 6 percent from saturates and not more than 10 percent from polyunsaturates. Medical researchers are cautious about recommending more than 10 percent polyunsaturates because the long-range effects of large amounts are unknown.

The AHA and the other organizations are concerned primarily with prevention of cardiovascular disease. The concern about fat and cancer is more recent and so it is not surprising that there is a dearth of guidelines. Dr. Ernest Wynder, who is concerned with the cancer problem, suggests guidelines similar to those of the AHA for prevention of both groups of diseases.

In later chapters we'll discuss daily food plans for lacto-vegetarians (those who eat dairy products) and vegans (those who eat only plant foods). The basic food plans for both types of

---

represents 44 percent of his calories. He would also get additional fat from other sources, including grains and beans. For a woman eating the Recommended Dietary Allowance of 2000 calories, the 1200 calories of fat would account for 60 percent of her diet.

---

diet are based on a maximum of 30 percent fat, including no more than 10 percent saturates and no more than 10 percent polyunsaturates.

The total amount of fat could have been set somewhat higher and still be within the AHA standard. The 30 percent level is a better target for two reasons: the experience of many vegetarians has shown that you can prepare very palatable meals within this guideline; and if you occasionally eat too much fat, you'll still average out below the AHA guideline of 35 percent. Whether 30 percent is healthier than 35 is impossible to say, but if you keep to the lower level as a target, you'll have more leeway for occasional high-fat dishes such as the gourmet recipes in Chapter 12.

It is possible that some people may benefit by cutting fat consumption to 25 or even 20 percent. You can do this easily within the basic plan simply by cutting down on margarine, butter, and other fatty foods.

## LIMITING SALT IN YOUR DIET

Most experts recommend that you limit salt consumption because there is evidence that it may cause high blood pressure, at least in some people. Ethnic groups such as the Eskimos, who eat less than 5 grams of salt per day (the equivalent of about one teaspoon), are free of hypertension, while the northern Japanese, who average more than 25 grams a day (about five teaspoons), have one of the highest rates of hypertension in the world. Salt is not the only suspected causal factor in hypertension. Obesity, heredity, and stress have also been implicated, and recent evidence suggests that caffeine and sugar play contributory roles.

Salt is not the only way to make foods palatable. Vinegar, mustard, horseradish, onions, lemon juice, bay leaves, sage, thyme, paprika, tarragon, marjoram, cloves, chives, garlic, pepper, and other herbs and spices are the basis of tasty cooking. Wherever you can, use these instead of salt.

## THE CHOLESTEROL PROBLEM

Over the years many experiments with human subjects have shown that increased cholesterol in the diet also raises the amount of cholesterol in the blood. Autopsies show that cholesterol is a major component of the fatty deposits that characterize atherosclerosis. Epidemiological studies have shown again and again that those with high levels of cholesterol in the blood are more prone to coronary heart disease than those with low levels. On the basis of this evidence the American Heart Association and many individual researchers recommend limiting the amount of cholesterol in the diet as a means of reducing the risk of coronary heart disease. Among vegetarian foods, this limitation would apply particularly to eggs, the most concentrated source of cholesterol among common foods.

Many highly respected researchers vigorously dispute the need for such restriction. They point out that the evidence for a causal link between dietary cholesterol and coronary heart disease has not been firmly established. Some, like Dr. Mark Altschule of the Harvard Medical School, see no solid evidence for a causal link between the level of cholesterol in the blood and atherosclerosis. Other researchers claim that most experiments indicating a relationship between blood cholesterol and dietary cholesterol have not simulated typical eating conditions. They point in particular to three new studies in which people were fed one or two whole eggs a day under much more normal conditions. In each of the studies, there was no change in the average blood cholesterol level over a period of several months. Some subjects experienced *lower* blood cholesterol levels, while others had higher levels, and still others experienced no change. In commenting on these tests, George Briggs, professor of nutritional science at the University of California, Berkeley, and his colleague, Jean Weinberger, state that "the great variation in response to eggs . . . emphasizes the desirability of evaluating dietary changes on an individual basis rather than assuming that a certain dietary component will automatically elevate blood cholesterol."

Eggs are not only the most concentrated source of cholesterol but also the most nutritious of all vegetarian foods. Their high-quality protein and high concentration of vitamins and minerals make them particularly valuable foods during growth and pregnancy. Fortunately, the concern over egg consumption centers primarily on adult males, the group most prone to coronary heart disease. The nutritionist Jean Mayer, for example, advises men to eat no more than two eggs a week. Other experts consider such advice absurdly restrictive.

While the nutritionists argue over the problem, there are two steps that egg lovers can take to protect themselves against possible risk. The first is to have periodic blood checks and then abide by the dietary advice of your physician. In this way you are more likely to benefit from the latest research developments regarding cholesterol. The second step is to engage in a regular program of exercise. Exercise not only has some effect in reducing the total blood cholesterol level but also, as we have noted, may raise blood levels of high-density lipoproteins, the cholesterol fraction that could have a protective effect against coronary heart disease. There is also evidence that regular exercise helps to lower blood pressure.

## HOW HEALTHY IS
## A VEGETARIAN DIET?

The most reliable information on the health value of vegetarian diets comes from a study of Seventh Day Adventists published in 1978. The Seventh Day Adventist Church, an evangelical Protestant denomination, recommends a lacto-vegetarian diet to its members. Vegetarianism is not mandatory, but half of the members practice it, and many of the rest eat meat only occasionally. A small number practice a vegan (no animal food) diet. Adventists don't smoke and don't drink alcohol, coffee, or tea, and they put emphasis on adequate exercise and other preventative health measures.

A group of researchers headed by Dr. Roland Philips of the Loma Linda University Department of Biostatistics and Epidemiology followed 24,044 California Adventists over a period of six years to determine their mortality from coronary heart disease (CHD). Their study provides comparative data on Adventist meat eaters, lacto-ovo vegetarians, and vegans, and compares these groups to the general California population:

### Standardized Mortality Ratios
### Coronary Heart Disease—Age 35 and Over

|  | Males | Females |
|---|---|---|
| General California population | 100 | 100 |
| Seventh Day Adventist meat eaters | 56 | 49 |
| Seventh Day Adventist lacto-vegetarians | 39 | 42 |
| Seventh Day Adventist vegans | 14 | 94 |

We would expect that Adventists as a group would be less apt to suffer CHD than other Californians because of their abstinence from tobacco and other healthy habits. This is borne out by the data above, which show considerably lower mortality from the disease among the Adventist groups. The more interesting comparison is among Adventists who differ in their dietary practices but who are reasonably similar with respect to other practices that might affect health. The data show that Adventist males who practice a lacto-vegetarian (or lacto-ovo-vegetarian) diet suffer significantly less CHD than their meat-eating brethren. Mortality for vegan males is even lower than that of lacto-vegetarians but the authors of the study suggest caution in interpreting the data for this particular group because of the small numbers involved.

The report provides additional information for male Adventists by age group. Among those thirty-five to sixty-four, the difference in CHD mortality between meat eaters and vegetarians is particularly striking: the meat eaters were three times more likely to die of CHD. Among males sixty-five and over, the meat eaters had about a 50 percent greater mortality from the disease than did the vegetarians.

The authors of the study point out that part of the difference in mortality is probably due to the poorer health of the meat eaters. They tended to weigh more, were more likely to have a prior history of hypertension and heart disease, and, at least among the elderly, were less likely to engage in exercise. They were also more likely to have diabetes, a risk factor in CHD. As the authors of the report note, it is possible that their diet may have promoted hypertension, obesity, and diabetes among the Adventist meat eaters. Dr. Philips and his colleagues, in assessing this information, concluded that vegetarianism "may have a significant influence on the risk of CHD deaths among males." (Their conclusion does not, of course, necessarily imply that you can't be just as healthy on a prudent omnivore diet containing comparable amounts of fat, protein, carbohydrate, and fiber. The !Kung bushmen of Botswana, for example, eat moderate amounts of meat and are virtually free of heart disease even in old age.)

The low incidence of CHD mortality for male vegetarians, and particularly for male vegans, is not surprising. Over the years, studies have shown that lacto-vegetarians have lower blood cholesterol levels than meat eaters and that vegans have lower levels still. The low blood cholesterol of vegetarians is largely explained by moderate consumption of saturated fat, high consumption of polyunsaturates, and, most probably, the lack of cholesterol in plant foods. There is also evidence that vegetable protein is associated with lower blood cholesterol levels. Another factor affecting heart disease is the unexplained tendency of vegetarians, and particularly vegans, to be leaner than meat eaters.* Lacto-vegetarians also tend to have lower blood pressure than meat eaters, and there is evidence that the blood pressure of vegans is the lowest of all. The reasons for the low blood pressure of vegetarians are not fully understood.†

## FEMALE VEGETARIANS
## AND HEART DISEASE

Female Adventists on a lacto-vegetarian (or lacto-ovo vegetarian) diet suffer virtually the same mortality from CHD as their meat-eating co-religionists. The authors of the study note that this was not unexpected because low blood cholesterol, one of the chief benefits of a vegetarian diet, "seems to have a questionable relationship to risk of CHD in females, particularly older females."

The CHD mortality of vegan famales—virtually the same as that of non-Adventist females in California—was unexpectedly

---

*A possible explanation for the apparent leanness of vegetarians may be the lower caloric density of most vegetarian foods. With the exception of fats, oils, and nuts, plant foods contain more water and less fat than animal foods, and thus vegetarians may satisfy their hunger pangs with fewer calories. On the other hand, there are some who have theorized that fiber, which is abundant in vegetarian and especially vegan diets, acts as a natural barrier to overeating. This theory has yet to be tested. Others have suggested that lack of vitamin B12 in plant foods is associated with the low weight of vegans, but Dr. T. A. B. Sanders, a British expert on veganism, found no relationship between the level of vitamin B12 in the blood and the proportion of body fat.

†Obesity is associated with high blood pressure, and it is therefore plausible that vegetarians, with their apparent tendency to leanness, would enjoy lower blood pressure levels than meat eaters. Several studies have suggested that the less animal food eaten, the lower the blood pressure will be. Another possible contributor to low blood pressure among vegetarians is suggested by an experiment showing that an increased P/S ratio (ratio of polyunsaturated fatty acid to saturated fatty acids) lowers the blood pressure of males. Lacto-vegetarians and, to a greater extent, vegans, normally eat a diet with a high P/S ratio.

high. Previous research had given no hint that vegan women might be any less healthy than lacto-vegetarian women. In attempting to explain this surprising finding, the authors speculate that vegans, being an extremely select and unusual group, may have some characteristics that increase their risk. Another possible explanation offered by the authors is that the female vegans might have some type of dietary deficiency that increases their risk. There could, of course, be a tendency for female Adventists who develop signs of CHD to switch to the vegan diet, but the researchers found no evidence that this occurred.

It is not clear whether the information on CHD mortality of Adventist vegan females indicates a health hazard for those who follow a balanced diet, such as that recommended in this book. At least until additional research on this point becomes available it is wise for vegan women to have regular health checkups with special attention given to factors that might predispose to CHD.

## VEGETARIANS AND CANCER

The Adventists, in addition to having less coronary heart disease, also have far less cancer than non-Adventists. This can be explained, in part, by their abstinence from smoking and drinking, which are related to cancer of the lung, mouth, esophagus, and bladder. They also—and this is the interesting part—have less cancer of the colon and stomach, types that are thought to be related to diet. Adventists usually eat less fat than most other Americans.

It would be easy to jump to the conclusion that the Seventh Day Adventist diet protects against some types of cancer. Unfortunately, we don't have comparative information on cancer mortality for Adventist vegetarians versus meat eaters. There is a study under way that may provide important clues to the value of the Adventist diet. This study, which is funded by the National Cancer Institute, is following 100,000 church members over a six-year period. It will attempt to relate type of diet and diet components, such as saturated fat, sugar, and fiber, to the rates for the various types of cancer. The report will not be available until some time in the 1980s.

There is some evidence suggesting that diet may not be the key contributor to the Adventists' low cancer mortality. The

Mormons, who are nonvegetarian but otherwise very similar to Adventists in their health habits, also have low mortality rates for types of cancer thought to be related to diet. Does this mean that there is some factor not related to diet that protects both the Adventists and the Mormons? We don't know the answer to this question—at least not yet.

## GETTING THE MOST OUT OF A VEGETARIAN DIET

The Seventh Day Adventist study shows that, at least for males, a vegetarian diet helps protect against coronary heart disease. There is a strong presumption that it does this by keeping blood cholesterol low, by helping to keep body weight down, and possibly also by keeping blood pressure low. Benefits such as these don't come automatically. They come in part from following sound guidelines such as those discussed earlier in this chapter. Benefits also come from maintaining proper balance of the various types of food and in avoiding certain pitfalls peculiar to vegetarianism. In the chapters that follow, we'll explore ways in which sound nutrition principles can be applied to lacto-vegetarian and vegan diets, not only for adults, but also for infants, adolescents, pregnant women, older people, and athletes.

# 2

## Vegetarian Diets
## for Adults

Recently a writer in *Mademoiselle* magazine claimed that "a major hazard in all vegetarian diets which severely restrict animal meats is the lack of sufficient complete proteins." She went on to say that "the nutritional elements in vegetables are so widely dispersed that packing all essential amino acids into each day's meals is tough for the most skilled cook."

If you analyze the recipes in any good vegetarian cookbook, you would see that this claim doesn't make sense. But let me demonstrate how easy it is to get adequate protein.

An average man needs 56 grams a day, according to the National Research Council, and this amount includes a 30 percent cushion to allow for individual variation. If you are a lacto-vegetarian, you will get 63 grams of protein simply by eating a cup of oatmeal, two slices of toast, a peanut butter sandwich, a cup of beans, two glasses of milk, and an ounce of cheese.

If you are on a vegan diet—all plant foods—you will get 58 grams of protein by eating a cup of oatmeal, two slices of toast, a peanut butter sandwich, a cup of beans, a cup of rice, an ounce of mixed nuts, and two glasses of soy milk.

Both lacto-vegetarians and vegans ordinarily get more than these amounts because there is substantial protein in many vegetables (such as broccoli) and desserts that contain milk or eggs (such as ice cream or custard).

It is important to distinguish between complete and incomplete protein. Milk and eggs contain complete protein and indeed the quality is actually higher than that in meat and poultry. Vegetarians who eat substantial amounts of dairy products or dairy products and eggs should have no problem in getting a sufficient amount of complete protein. Plant proteins are usually classified as incomplete but certain combinations of plant foods such as beans and grains provide complete protein when taken at the same meal. The enhancement of protein value through combining foods is important particularly for vegans during growth and pregnancy. In Chapter 8 we will take a closer look at this phenomenon of protein combinations.

## DO YOU RISK VITAMIN OR MINERAL DEFICIENCIES ON A VEGETARIAN DIET?

If you look at Appendix 1, you'll see that typical vegetarian menus for adults supply adequate vitamins and minerals as measured against the Recommended Dietary Allowances. The only important exception to this is in the case of vegans, who ordinarily don't get adequate vitamin B12 unless they take a supplement. (Later in this chapter we will explore in more detail the special problems of vegans.)

Iron-deficiency anemia is a common problem among women of childbearing age, and it is possible that many vegetarians suffer from it. Theoretically, vegetarians should be particularly at risk because iron from plant foods is less well absorbed than that from meat. Milk has little iron but beans, dried fruit, and some vegetables have fairly large amounts. (See Appendix 6.) The iron in eggs is particularly valuable because it is more readily absorbed than that in plant foods. Vitamin C greatly increases the absorption of iron from other foods while tea and, to a lesser extent, coffee inhibits absorption. Possibly because they include citrus fruits and vegetables rich in vitamin C in their meals, many women on vegetarian diets have no deficiency symptoms and according to Dr. F. R. Ellis, a British expert on vegetarian nutrition, vegans have fewer deficiency symptoms than omnivores. If you follow a high-nutrition diet such as that suggested in the following pages, you'll minimize the chance of being deficient. If you are concerned, consult your doctor. He will recommend a supplement if it is needed.

In recent years there has been some concern that many Americans suffer from a marginal deficiency of zinc, which can retard wound healing and decrease your ability to taste and smell. Some nutritionists are concerned that vegetarians may get less zinc than omnivores because plant foods are not as good sources as meat, and because fiber and a substance called phytic acid may inhibit absorption of the mineral. Two recent American studies on the zinc status of vegetarians are inconclusive but suggest possible deficiencies. On the other hand Dr. Ellis has found evidence that zinc values of British vegans are within the normal range. Marginal zinc deficiency is not a major hazard for normally healthy adults. If you have wounds that are slow to heal or have problems with tasting and smelling, you should of course see your physician and discuss your diet with him.

# BEGINNING ON
# A VEGETARIAN DIET

Before getting into specific food recommendations, let's take a brief look at the problems that a beginning vegetarian is apt to have. There are three things to watch out for.

The first has to do with timing. For most people, it's wise to get into a vegetarian diet gradually. Many people first give up beef, veal, and pork, then chicken and turkey and, finally, seafood, at each step substituting more dairy products, eggs, beans, vegetables, grains, and other plant food. If you change too abruptly you may suffer temporary digestive disturbances because your system may not adjust quickly to the substantial increase in dietary fiber. Set your own pace in changing over. Some people can change abruptly without ill effect, but others need weeks or even months.

The second thing has to do with chewing. Fruits, whole grains, and raw vegetables—essentials of a good vegetarian diet—take a lot more chewing than meat and white bread. Besides being important for healthy teeth, thorough chewing stimulates secretion of saliva and gastric juice, which aid digestion. It also helps the intestine to absorb nutrients more readily. If you want to get the full benefit of a vegetarian diet, take the time to chew thoroughly.

The third and most important thing for the beginning vegetarian is learning how to choose the right foods. Everyone—meat eaters and vegetarians alike—should try to get variety in their diets. Variety is important because it reduces the chance of a deficiency in any one nutrient. As a vegetarian, you are limiting your choices and so it's wise to be conscious of the possibilities for variety within the vegetarian food groups. Vegans in particular should be conscious of the importance of variety in their meal planning.

## LACTO-VEGETARIAN DIETS

What kinds of foods are best for lacto-vegetarians? Good diets for healthy adults are usually based on a balance of foods from five groups: vegetables, fruits, grains, beans-nuts-seeds, and dairy products-eggs.

The suggested servings of the five basic foods shown in Table 1 are intended to give you a general idea of the right proportions you'll need for getting a good balance of nutrients. There is nothing sacred about these amounts but it's wise to get the suggested minimum servings of dairy products or eggs as these are your only natural source of vitamin B12. If you get less than the suggested servings from this group, compensate by taking a B12 supplement or a nutritional yeast fortified with B12.

The suggested servings are for people in the average weight range—140 to 170 pounds for males and 110 to 145 pounds for women. If your lean or ideal weight is considerably more or less than these average ranges, adjust your servings accordingly. If your physical activity is much greater than average, you would want to eat additional servings.

If you want to see how the basic food groups work out in practice, turn to Appendix 1, which shows nutrients in typical vegetarian menus.

# CONTROLLING FAT ON A
# LACTO-VEGETARIAN DIET

The basic foods in Table 1 supply about 60 percent of the total calories that you'll need. You'll also want to eat fats and oils and a certain amount of other foods including snacks and desserts.

In Chapter 1 we talked about the desirability of keeping total fat calories to 30 percent, and limiting saturates and polyunsaturates to 10 percent each. You can do this by limiting your consumption of fatty foods, including fats and oils, whole milk, cheese, nuts, and fatty desserts. If you are an adult male, limit

---

**TABLE 1**

**Daily Food Guide for Lacto-Vegetarian Adults**

| Food Group | Suggested Minimum Servings | |
|---|---|---|
| Vegetables | 2 | Eat a dark green or deep yellow vegetable at least three times a week to get vitamin A. Fresh or frozen are preferable to canned. Eat at least 1 raw vegetable or salad every day. Serving sizes are usually 1 cup. (See Appendix 6.) |
| Fruits | 2 | Can be taken as juice, whole fruit, or dried fruit, but whole fruit is better. Women may want to include one of the iron-rich fruits or juices—raisins, prune, apricot—several times a week. |
| Grains | 4 (3 for women) | A serving is 2 slices of bread, 1 cup of rice (cooked) or hot breakfast cereal, 2 ounces of ready-to-eat breakfast cereal, ⅔ cup spaghetti (cooked), or 4–6 crackers. Include at least some whole-grain cereals. |
| Beans and Nuts | 2 | A serving of beans is 1 cup (cooked) or 1 portion of any of the bean recipes in Chapter 11. A serving of nuts or seeds is 2 ounces, or 4 tablespoons of nut butter. In combination with cereals, beans supply high-quality protein. Nuts and seeds are less valuable than beans because they are high in fat. |
| Dairy Products and Eggs | 3 | A serving is 1 cup of whole milk, skim milk, yogurt, 1 ounce of cheese, or 1 egg. These are your only natural sources of vitamin B12. Don't rely exclusively on cheese to satisfy your requirement as it is high in fat and low in vitamin B12. |

---

your daily consumption to eight portions of the foods listed below. If you are female, don't eat more than 6 portions.*

| FOOD | PORTION |
|---|---|
| Whole milk | 1 cup |
| Cheese (except low-fat, such as cottage) | 1 ounce |
| Nuts and seeds | ½ ounce or 1 tablespoon nut butter |
| Salad oil | 2 teaspoons |
| Mayonnaise | 2 teaspoons |
| Salad dressing, commercial | 1 tablespoon |
| Margarine or butter | 2 pats (= ⅓ ounce) |
| Eggs | 1 |
| Soybeans (other beans are low in fat) | 1 cup cooked |
| High-fat sauces | 1 portion (See Table 2 for list.) |
| High-fat snacks and desserts | 1 portion (See Table 2 for list.) |
| Gourmet vegetarian entrees† | 1 portion (See Table 2 for list.) |

To keep within the guidelines for saturates and polyunsaturates, use margarine and salad oils based on corn oil, safflower oil, soybean oil, and cottonseed oil. If you regularly use butter instead of margarine, you are likely to exceed the guidelines for saturated fat. You can stay within the guidelines and still use butter if you don't eat fatty desserts or snacks.

* The suggested amounts of fatty food for males are calculated as follows: 1) recommended calorie consumption for average-size male is 2700; 2) 30 percent in fat = 90 grams; 3) total fat in recommended low-fat portion of diet averages about 20 grams, leaving about 70 grams to be chosen from fatty foods; 4) listed fatty foods average about 9 grams per portion; 5) 70 grams ÷ 9 grams = 8 portions of fatty foods. The recommended calorie consumption for women is 75 percent of that for males; hence suggested portions of fatty food for women is 6. If your ideal weight is more or less than average, you can adjust your consumption of fatty and nonfatty food accordingly in order to stay within the guideline for fat consumption.

† Many are extremely high in fat. Those who want to keep within the guidelines for fat consumption should put these dishes in the occasional treat class or cut down drastically on consumption of other fats.

If you want to cut the proportion of fat in your diet below 30 percent, you can do this simply by cutting down on the fatty foods listed on the preceding page. If, for example, the goal is 20 percent, males should limit themselves to five portions and females to 3 portions of the fatty foods.

Keeping within the guidelines for fat is not difficult after you've familiarized yourself with the basic principles. After a week or so the procedure will be virtually automatic.

## VEGAN DIETS

At one time vegan diets were considered quite risky because some adherents had serious health problems, including nervous disorders. After World War II it became apparent that the primary problem was lack of vitamin B12, a nutrient not ordinarily available from plant foods. By 1975, the evidence for the safety of the vegan diet was so apparent that it received the blessing of the National Academy of Sciences, an organization not known for nutritional radicalism. The NAS stresses that vegans should do two things: (a) supplement their diets with vitamin B12; and (b) get a variety of plant foods.

Within these guidelines, successful vegan diets can vary widely. At The Farm, a vegan commune in Tennessee, the emphasis is on beans. In California, vegans eat large amounts of fruit, while those in England tend to eat more cereals and nuts. One of the most extreme vegan diets is practiced by Buddhist monks in Korea, who consume more than 60 percent of their calories in the form of white rice. Despite this, they maintain apparent good health by also eating soy products and a variety of vegetables and fruits. They also benefit by not eating junk foods.

Some vegans don't enjoy good health because their meals depend too heavily on low-nutrition foods. The natives of Central Celebes, for example, get 82 percent of their calories from rice and 11 percent from coconut; certain poor Javanese get 95 percent of their calories from cassava root; and Papuan highlanders get 90 percent of their calories from sweet potatoes. Another example is the impoverished Indians from Madras, Travancore, and other areas of the subcontinent, who eat some beans, vegetables, and fruits, but not enough to make up for the unbalanced nutrition of white rice, which accounts for most of their calories. In America, people on macrobiotic diets have suffered severe nutritional problems because they ate little else but brown rice.

25

## TABLE 2
### Composition of Selected Foods*

| | Cal-ories | Pro-tein (g) | Fat (g) | Carbo-hydrates (g) |
|---|---|---|---|---|
| *Dairy Products and Eggs* | | | | |
| Whole milk, 1 cup | 160 | 9 | 9 | 12 |
| Skim milk, 1 cup | 90 | 9 | t | 12 |
| Cheddar cheese, 1 ounce | 115 | 7 | 9 | 1 |
| Cottage cheese, ½ cup | 120 | 15 | 5 | 3 |
| Uncreamed cottage cheese, ½ cup | 60 | 12 | t | 2 |
| Heavy cream, 1 tablespoon | 45 | t | 5 | 1 |
| Egg, 1 (large) | 80 | 6 | 6 | t |
| Sour cream, 2 tablespoons | 50 | t | 4 | 2 |
| *Fats and Oils* | | | | |
| Butter, 1 teaspoon (1 pat) | 35 | t | 4 | t |
| Margarine, 1 teaspoon (1 pat) | 35 | t | 4 | t |
| Salad or cooking oil, 1 teaspoon | 40 | 0 | 5 | 0 |
| Vegetable shortening, 1 tablespoon | 110 | 0 | 13 | 0 |
| Mayonnaise, 1 teaspoon | 35 | t | 4 | t |
| Store-bought salad dressing, 1 tablespoon | 65 | t | 6 | 2 |
| *Dairy Food Substitutes* | | | | |
| Soy milk, homemade, 1 cup (Recipe 36) | 135 | 8 | 8 | 8 |
| Soy milk, homemade, 1 cup made without oil (Recipe 36) | 95 | 8 | 3 | 9 |
| Soy milk, commercial, 1 cup (typical value) | 135 | 6 | 6 | 14 |
| Soy margarine, homemade, 1 teaspoon (Recipe 37) | 35 | t | 4 | t |
| Soy cheese, 1 ounce (Recipe 38) | 145 | 3 | 12 | 7 |
| Soy mayonnaise, 1 tablespoon (Recipe 39) | 31 | 1 | 3 | 1 |
| Soy whipped topping, 2 tablespoons whipped (Recipe 40) | 90 | 1 | 8 | 4 |
| Soy sour cream, 2 tablespoons (Recipe 41) | 50 | 1 | 3 | 5 |
| *High-Fat Snacks and Desserts* | | | | |
| Malted milk made with whole milk, 1 cup | 275 | 13 | 11 | 32 |

* Where recipes are indicated, see Part Two.

TABLE 2   (Continued)

| | Cal-<br>ories | Pro-<br>tein<br>(g) | Fat<br>(g) | Carbo-<br>hydrates<br>(g) |
|---|---|---|---|---|
| Malted milk made with ½ cup<br>  ice cream, 1 cup | 290 | 11 | 13 | 32 |
| Malted milk made with soy<br>  milk, 1 cup | 250 | 10 | 9 | 34 |
| High-protein drink made with<br>  soy milk, 1 cup (Recipe 29) | 210 | 11 | 7 | 26 |
| Ice cream, ½ cup | 130 | 3 | 7 | 14 |
| Sundae, ½ cup ice cream, ½<br>  ounce chocolate syrup | 175 | 3 | 8 | 26 |
| Soy milk ice cream, ½ cup<br>  (Recipe 42) | 145 | 3 | 7 | 19 |
| Custard, baked, ½ cup (made<br>  with eggs) | 150 | 7 | 7 | 15 |
| Chocolate pudding, ½ cup<br>  (made without eggs) | 190 | 4 | 6 | 33 |
| Pound cake, 3½ × 3 × ½<br>  inches (made with eggs) | 140 | 2 | 9 | 14 |
| Doughnuts, plain, 2 (made<br>  with eggs) | 200 | 2 | 9 | 26 |
| Fruitcake, ¾ × 2 × 1½ inches<br>  (made without eggs) | 165 | 2 | 7 | 26 |
| Layer cake, frosting, ¹/₁₆ of<br>  9-inch cake (made without<br>  egg yolk) | 275 | 3 | 10 | 45 |
| Brownie, 2 × 2 × 1 inches<br>  (made without eggs) | 145 | 2 | 9 | 15 |
| Oatmeal cookies, 4  2⅝ inches<br>  (made with egg) | 235 | 3 | 8 | 38 |
| Apple pie, ¹/₁₂ of 9-inch pie | 200 | 2 | 9 | 30 |
| Pancakes, 3  4-inch, 2<br>  tablespoons syrup, 1 pat<br>  margarine (made with eggs) | 335 | 6 | 14 | 46 |
| Cocoa, 1 cup | 175 | 7 | 9 | 20 |
| Nuts, ½ ounce or 1 tablespoon<br>  nut butter | 90 | 4 | 8 | 3 |
| Nut and raisin dip, ½ cup<br>  (Recipe 31) | 260 | 8 | 10 | 35 |
| Garlic dip, ½ cup (Recipe 32) | 145 | 5 | 7 | 16 |
| Date-nut dip, ½ cup (Recipe<br>  33) | 275 | 4 | 8 | 47 |
| Hummus, ½ cup (Recipe 34) | 185 | 8 | 9 | 20 |
| Blue cheese dip, ½ cup (Recipe<br>  35) | 220 | 14 | 10 | 20 |

| | Cal-ories | Pro-tein (g) | Fat (g) | Carbo-hydrates (g) |
|---|---|---|---|---|
| **TABLE 2** (Continued) | | | | |
| *Low-Fat Snacks and Desserts* | | | | |
| Malted milk made with skim milk, 1 cup | 205 | 13 | 2 | 32 |
| High-protein drink made with skim milk, 1 cup (Recipe 28) | 150 | 12 | 1 | 27 |
| Fruitshake, 1 cup (Recipe 30) | 135 | 2 | 0.5 | 33 |
| Yogurt, plain, 1 cup | 125 | 8 | 4 | 13 |
| Yogurt, flavored, 1 cup | 230 | 7 | 3 | 44 |
| Ice milk, ½ cup | 65 | 3 | 3 | 15 |
| Sherbet, 1 cup | 260 | 2 | 2 | 59 |
| Cupcake, 2½-inch-diameter, no icing | 90 | 1 | 3 | 14 |
| Popcorn, 2 cups, lightly oiled | 80 | 2 | 4 | 10 |
| Fruit and fruit juice (average portion) | 50–120 | low | low | high |
| *Low-Fat Entrees, per Serving\** | | | | |
| Basic bean and grain casserole (Recipe 1) | 270 | 13 | 6 | 43 |
| Bean burgers (Recipe 2) | 260 | 17 | 6 | 38 |
| Bean-nut roast (Recipe 3) | 320 | 16 | 8 | 46 |
| Old-fashioned baked beans (Recipe 4) | 285 | 16 | 1 | 54 |
| Basic bean soup (Recipe 5) | 300 | 18 | 1 | 57 |
| Fried beans and rice (Recipe 6) | 400 | 11 | 7 | 73 |
| Beans and pasta (Recipe 7) | 360 | 16 | 6 | 61 |
| Vegetable casserole (Recipe 8) | 250 | 16 | 5 | 35 |
| *Gourmet Vegetarian Entrees per Serving\** | | | | |
| Mushroom omelette (Recipe 9) | 290 | 14 | 23 | 5 |
| Spanish omelette (Recipe 10) | 320 | 16 | 23 | 12 |
| Cheddar cheese soufflé (Recipe 11) | 370 | 19 | 25 | 17 |
| Eggplant parmigiana (Recipe 12) | 250 | 14 | 18 | 12 |
| Mushroom quiche (Recipe 13) | 380 | 9 | 31 | 21 |
| Onion and blue cheese quiche (Recipe 14) | 245 | 8 | 17 | 15 |

\* Serving size indicated in Part Two. Where recipes are based on beans, it is assumed that low-fat beans are used. If made with soybeans, values for calories, protein, and fat will be higher.

| | Cal-ories | Pro-tein (g) | Fat (g) | Carbo-hydrates (g) |
|---|---|---|---|---|
| TABLE 2 (Continued) | | | | |
| Vegetable quiche (Recipe 15) | 210 | 10 | 12 | 16 |
| Bean rarebit (Recipe 16) | 415 | 27 | 17 | 43 |
| Lasagna (Recipe 17) | 310 | 19 | 10 | 36 |
| Ratatouille (Recipe 18) | 225 | 5 | 14 | 22 |
| *Sauces* | | | | |
| Bean sauce, 4 tablespoons (Recipe 19) | 110 | 5 | 4 | 14 |
| Cottage cheese sauce, 4 tablespoons (Recipe 20) | 50 | 5 | 1 | 4 |
| Béchamel sauce, 4 tablespoons (Recipe 21) | 115 | 4 | 8 | 8 |
| Sour cream sauce, 4 tablespoons (Recipe 22) | 155 | 4 | 11 | 8 |
| Egg sauce, 4 tablespoons (Recipe 23) | 125 | 4 | 10 | 5 |
| Mornay sauce, 4 tablespoons (Recipe 24) | 140 | 5 | 10 | 7 |
| Cheddar cheese sauce, 4 tablespoons (Recipe 25) | 175 | 10 | 12 | 6 |
| Mock Hollandaise sauce, 4 tablespoons (Recipe 26) | 105 | 4 | 8 | 4 |
| Blue cheese sauce, 4 tablespoons (Recipe 27) | 105 | 6 | 8 | 4 |

As a vegan, you must get virtually all your nutrients from four basic groups: vegetables, fruits, grains, and beans-nuts. A proper balance of these foods, such as the suggested amounts shown in Table 3, provides good nutrition.

You'll notice that in the table under "beans," it's suggested that you drink at least one cup a day of soy milk fortified with vitamin B12. This is the easiest way to get this nutrient, which isn't normally present in plant foods. Many commercial soy milks do not contain adequate vitamin B12. Choose one that contains at least 2 micrograms per cup. If you use a commercial product that has less, grind up a vitamin B12 tablet and add it to the soy milk. Some nutritional yeasts are fortified with B12. If none of your food is fortified with this vitamin, take a supplement. Be wary of taking vitamin C in large quantities (500 milligrams or more) as it may destroy vitamin B12. Megadoses of vitamin C have no proved value in preventing the common cold or any other malady.

| Food Group | Suggested Minimum Servings | |
|---|---|---|
| | | **TABLE 3** |
| | | **Daily Food Guide for Vegan Adults** |
| Vegetables | 4 (3 for women) | Eat at least 1 dark green leafy vegetable every day. They are your best natural sources of calcium (spinach is a major exception), riboflavin, and vitamin A. Eat at least 1 raw vegetable or salad every day. Serving sizes are usually 1 cup. (See Appendix 6.) |
| Fruits | 3 | Can be taken as juice or whole fruit but whole fruit is better. Women may want to include one of the iron-rich fruits or juices—raisin, prune, apricot—several times a week. |
| Grains | 5 (4 for women) | A serving is 2 slices of bread, 1 cup of rice (cooked) or hot breakfast cereal, 2 ounces of ready-to-eat breakfast cereal, ⅔ cup spaghetti (cooked), or 4–6 crackers. Include at least some whole-grain cereals. |
| Beans and Nuts (including soy milk) | 3 (2 for women) | A serving of beans is 1 cup (cooked) or 2 cups of soy milk, or 6 ounces of tofu (fermented soybean curd), or 1 portion of any of the bean recipes in Chapter 11, or 2 ounces of nuts, or 4 tablespoons of nut butter. A meal combining beans with cereals or nuts forms the protein base of vegan diets. Nuts and seeds are less valuable than beans because they are high in fat. It's wise to drink at least 1 cup of fortified soybean milk every day as this is the easiest way to get vitamin B12. |

In Appendix 1, you'll find typical menus based on the suggested amounts from the four food groups. The experience of many vegans throughout the world shows that you can deviate from the suggested amounts and still maintain excellent health. There is one lesson, however, that comes out of their experience: vegans thrive by sticking to the four basic food groups and by avoiding extreme emphasis on one particular type of food. There are cases of vegans who apparently thrive on less than the four basic groups, but there is no benefit in cutting out any of them. By choosing the widest possible variety, you'll increase the chances of getting adequate amounts of all nutrients, including, perhaps, some that have not yet been discovered.

One other point about variety: within the four basic groups, try to get as many different foods as you can. Try new vegetables—you might like some of the unusual ones such as okra or collards. Try new grains—raw millet makes a good breakfast cereal if you don't mind a lot of chewing. Try tahini (sesame butter) or cashew butter in place of peanut butter. By doing this you not only improve your chances of getting better nutrition, you also avoid the possibility of eating too much of one food that may contain toxic substances—pesticides, for example; or aflatoxins, which are produced by molds on some nuts.

If you're new to the vegan diet, you're probably wondering what you can use in place of mayonnaise, cream, butter, and margarine. Most margarines contain nonfat dry milk, but a few brands with no animal ingredients are available in health-food stores. Like most health-food-store items, they're much more expensive than the corresponding supermarket items. Over the years, ingenious vegans have worked out homemade recipes for margarine and other fat and oil products. You'll find these in Chapter 14.

Most vegans work into the diet slowly because it takes time to acclimate the taste buds to a whole new set of sensations. One of the chief difficulties, at least for tea and coffee drinkers, is in giving up milk, for soy milk often ruins the flavor of their favorite beverage. If this is the case with you, try different brands, and if this doesn't work, experiment with homemade soy milk. In Chapter 14, you'll find a recipe for soy milk that may suit you as a coffee "creamer." Frozen liquid creamers are usually plant based but the powdered creamers (and also the frozen whipped toppings) include sodium caseinate (milk protein).

One strategy in adjusting to vegan food is to develop a talent for cooking interesting dishes. Fortunately, there are now several cookbooks devoted to the special problems of vegan cooking (see Appendix 5) and in Part II of this book you will find some no-fuss recipes for vegan dishes.

A technique that seems to work for some people is to fast for a day or two—no more except under medical supervision—before going on a vegan diet. You're so hungry at the end of the fast that your new diet is likely to be inviting.

## THE CONTROVERSY
## OVER VITAMIN B12

Vitamin B12 is essential in the formation of DNA. Lack of this vitamin in the diet may lead to infertility in females, nervous disorders, and megaloblastic anemia. Infertility due to lack of vitamin B12 is reversible if the vitamin is taken.

Nervous disorders are a far more serious consequence of dietary vitamin B12 deficiency. The early symptoms include a tingling sensation in the extremities, followed by loss of the sense of touch. If these symptoms are not reversed by taking vitamin B12, the disorder gets worse. The later symptoms include a condition called *subacute combined degeneration of the spinal cord*, which will result in permanent injury and even death if countermeasures are not taken.

In megaloblastic anemia abnormally large red blood cells are formed and distribution of oxygen to the tissues is reduced, resulting in severe lethargy. The symptoms of anemia are to a certain extent alleviated by ingesting folic acid, a vitamin normally abundant in the vegan diet.

Many vegans insist that they do not need to supplement their diet with B12. On the other hand, all responsible medical authorities agree that it is desirable to add B12 to the vegan diet. Why this difference of opinion?

The difference arises largely because the consequences of vitamin B12 deficiency are rare and slow to appear. The body normally contains sufficient B12 to last three years or more without replenishment. In addition, the symptoms of megaloblastic anemia, as we have seen, are suppressed by folic acid. It's also possible that some vegans get sufficient B12 by ingesting microorganisms or other contaminants that produce the vitamin. For example, impoverished Pakistanis and Asians in East Africa get adequate B12 although they eat few or no animal products. The vitamin can be synthesized by microorganisms present in fecal matter and so can find its way into their food supply or well water. When Pakistanis on a vegan diet move to Britain, where hygiene is better, some develop deficiency symptoms.

Some vegans in America and Europe get a certain amount of vitamin B12 from seaweed. Seaweed grown near sewage often contains small amounts of the vitamin but is an unreliable source. According to one report, red seaweeds average about one microgram of B12 per teaspoon, equivalent to a third of the Recommended Dietary Allowance. The concentration may vary seasonally by a factor of ten, and furthermore the vitamin is not stable in oxygen and light.

Although there are a few reported cases of vegans who have survived for up to twenty years or more in good health without *apparent* ingestion of vitamin B12, it is unwise not to take a supplement because of the possibly drastic health consequences. Dr. Frey Ellis, the British expert on vegan nutrition and consultant hematologist at Kingston Hospital near London, advises vegans to either eat foods that are fortified with the vitamin (such as soy milk or nutritional yeast) or take a B12 capsule. Dr. Ellis urges those who insist that they don't need a supplement to have their blood checked at least once a year, or preferably every six months. Supplementation with B12 does not violate vegan principles, since the vitamin is grown in a vegetable medium.

## CONTROLLING FAT ON A VEGAN DIET

Vegans typically get 30 percent of their calories as fat, with about 5 percent in saturates and somewhat more than 10 percent in polyunsaturates. (The balance is in monounsaturates.) The guideline for polyunsaturated fat is 10 percent. If you want to keep close to this guideline, don't overemphasize fats and oils that are extremely high in polyunsaturates, such as corn or safflower oil and soft margarine.* You may, at least part of the time, want to use fats and oils that have low or moderate amounts of polyunsaturates, such as peanut or olive oil and regular margarine.

Vegans don't normally have a problem in controlling the total amount of fat in their diets. If you are concerned about fat, limit your consumption according to the suggestions for lacto-vegetarians on page 24.

## HOW DO YOU GET
## ENOUGH CALCIUM WITHOUT MILK?

How do vegans get enough calcium without milk or other dairy products? Milk, one of the richest sources of the mineral,

---

* Dr. T. A. B. Sanders has suggested that vegans may not be subject to the possibly adverse effect of large amounts of polyunsaturated fatty acids because of the high fiber content of their diet. Polyunsaturated fatty acids are known to result in greater secretion of bile salts than saturated or monounsaturated fatty acids. Degradation of bile salts in the bowel may produce carcinogens. The fiber, according to the hypothesis, minimizes the degradation of bile salts in the bowel by promoting rapid excretion. Thus, large amounts of polyunsaturated oils may be less deleterious in high-fiber diets such as that of the vegans. Because this subject needs further research before more definite judgments can be made, I have, in the recommendations for vegans, adhered to the American Heart Association guideline of 10 percent maximum polyunsaturated fatty acids in the diet.

provides 36 percent of the Recommended Dietary Allowance (RDA) in an 8-ounce glass. Most beans provide 12 percent or less of the RDA in an average serving, while cereals, fruits, and most nuts and seeds provide even lower amounts. Carrageenan (Irish moss), whole sesame seeds, and a few vegetables, such as broccoli, collards, kale, and spinach, contain large amounts. In some vegetables, including spinach, the calcium is not available to the body because it binds with a substance called oxalic acid. (Vegetables high in oxalic acid are indicated in Appendix 6.) On the basis of these facts, should we conclude that vegans get insufficient calcium? The answer may depend on which calcium allowance you use. The allowance recommended by the National Academy of Sciences (NAS) for adults is 800 milligrams while the World Health Organization (WHO) sets its level at only 400 to 500 milligrams. Many countries, including Great Britain, adhere to the WHO standard. WHO bases its standard on studies which show that people adapt successfully to levels as low as 200 to 400 milligrams per day. NAS notes that these studies were done in tropical or semitropical areas with abundant sunlight. Sunlight supplies vitamin D, which greatly aids the absorption of calcium.

Adult vegans ordinarily have no problem in exceeding the WHO allowance, while males may even exceed the higher NAS allowance. This is because most foods in the four basic groups contain moderate amounts and thus the total calcium can be substantial.

Should you as an adult vegan be concerned if you get less calcium than the NAS allowance of 800 milligrams a day? The answer is not clear. There is a recent study indicating that adults, particularly older ones, may need as much as 800 milligrams or more a day. On the other hand, calcium requirements are based on the needs of omnivores, who, as a group, consume far more protein than vegans. On the typical high-protein omnivore diet, loss of calcium through excretion is higher than on the moderate-protein diet of most vegans. Because it is not entirely certain whether calcium is a problem nutrient, particularly for those over fifty, we will discuss it further in Chapter 6, which deals with the problems of older vegetarians.

Actually, it's easy to exceed the RDA merely by drinking two or three glasses of calcium-fortified soy milk. Most commercial soy milks are fortified. You can easily add calcium (and other nutrients) to homemade soy milk (see Chapter 14). If you make your own bread, you can fortify it with calcium by adding a teaspoon of calcium carbonate (purified chalk) to each pound of flour. Calcium carbonate is available from any pharmacist.

# WILL YOU GET ENOUGH OF THE OTHER VITAMINS AND MINERALS ON A VEGAN DIET?

Plant foods are naturally devoid of vitamin D, but some brands of margarine are fortified with this nutrient. It is not essential, at least for adults, to get the vitamin in food because it is produced in the skin by the ultraviolet rays of the sun. Glass filters out ultraviolet rays, but you'll get some in the shade of a tree. The adult requirement for vitamin D is so small that it is probably satisfied by casual outdoor exposure; and if you've been brought up as an omnivore or a lacto-vegetarian, you'll have large stores of vitamin D in your liver to draw upon. In extreme cases, the lack of vitamin D in the diet, in combination with a lack of sunlight, can lead to osteomalacia (adult rickets). This is unlikely to happen unless you're bedridden for an extended period. (In that case, your doctor might advise taking a vitamin D supplement.) Infants and small children have a greater need for vitamin D than adults. We'll cover their needs in the next chapter.

At least one report has suggested that vegans may be deficient in riboflavin. Although vegans have fewer concentrated sources of the vitamin than lacto-vegetarians, there have been no reports of symptoms due to a deficiency. Among vegan foods, green leafy vegetables and fortified soy milk are good sources. A deficiency causes reddened lips, cracks at the corners of the mouth, and sores on the eye, but fortunately is unlikely to cause severe illness.

# VEGAN DIETS WITHOUT SOY MILK

One of the sticking points on a vegan diet is soy milk, for many people find that they can't get used to the taste. If you don't drink soy milk, it's wise to eat an extra helping of green leafy vegetables to replace each glass. This will help protect you against possible deficiencies of calcium and riboflavin.

# VEGAN DIETS IN WEIGHT LOSS

If you go on a vegan diet to lose weight, you can increase the chances of success by getting regular exercise—say, an hour of vigorous walking or an hour of tennis a day. We have within us a mechanism that keeps a balance between the amount of calories we get from food and the amount of calories we expend in living. The mechanism apparently does not work well for very sedentary people. Jean Mayer, the former Harvard nutritionist, illustrated this in an experiment with rats. Rats who exercised from one to six hours a day maintained normal weight, but those who exercised less than an hour became overweight. Overweight people should, of course, consult their doctors before engaging in a program of vigorous exercise.

Anyone who is overweight knows that it's easier to lose pounds than to keep your weight down once you've reached a normal level. Many people go on crash diets and then, when they've reached their weight goal, revert to their old eating habits and so gain back the lost pounds. If you adopt a vegan diet for weight reduction, your chances of keeping slim will be greater if you stay with the diet permanently or add only low-fat dairy products and a moderate number of eggs.

# 3

# Vegetarian Diets
# for Infants

If you want good advice on which foods are best, ask your own infant! This is not as fanciful as it sounds, for there is a well-known experiment that suggests that the leading experts on child nutrition are the children themselves.

More than forty years ago, Dr. Clara Davis of Children's Memorial Hospital in Chicago decided to find out what foods infants would eat if the choice was up to them. She took fifteen children, ages six to eleven months, who had never tasted solid food and gave them their choice of a large variety of wholesome dishes. The foods included cow's milk, fruit, fruit juices, vegetables, eggs, whole grains, beef, lamb, chicken, fish, liver, bone marrow, and brains. In all, thirty-four different foods were offered to the infants every day. None was seasoned, but salt was provided as a separate item. No sugar or high-fat products, such as cream, butter, or cheese, were included. Nuts and beans were also excluded. The nurses who administered the feeding were instructed to let the infants choose on their own and not to show either approval or disapproval of the choices.

The fifteen children thrived on the diet. None had any serious illness during the six years of the experiment while some who started out malnourished or with rickets soon became well on the diet. All ate just enough to maintain proper weight. After six months, none was noticeably too thin or too fat even though they were allowed to eat as little or as much as they wanted.

At the beginning of the experiment the infants chose foods at random, but after a few weeks they settled on several favorites and ignored others. They all chose different combinations and changed their foods unpredictably. Often they had odd combinations, such as a breakfast of orange juice and liver or a supper of eggs, bananas, and milk.

This was obviously not a vegetarian experiment, but it has important lessons for both omnivore and vegetarian parents. It suggests the wisdom of offering a variety of foods and allowing the infant to make the choice. You don't, of course, have to offer thirty-four different foods to your child every day, but from time to time he can be offered new foods. If you use adult foods that have been specially pureed or chopped rather than rely on packaged baby food, the cost of the rejected food is minimal.

The study also suggests the importance of restricting your child's choices to wholesome foods. Dr. Davis tried to approximate the diet of primitive peoples by including no refined sugar and no seasonings. You yourself undoubtedly have an acquired taste for these foods, but your child does not, nor does he have a nutritional need for any of them.

Dr. Davis also excluded vegetable oils and processed dairy products, such as cheese, butter, and cream. There is no medical reason to exclude moderate amounts of fatty products. Although the experts are concerned about obesity in childhood, they're not ready to recommend elimination of all fat and oil products from the diet. About 50 percent of the calories in breast milk (and most formulas) is from fat and so the experts are understandably cautious about radically changing the proportion during weaning. One expert recommends against infant diets with less than 30 percent of total calories in fat because nutritional imbalances may result. The typical vegetarian menus for the six- to twelve-month age group shown in Appendix 1 contain over 35 percent fat.

It's wise to avoid jams, jellies, puddings made with cornstarch, and fruits canned in heavy syrup as these provide too much sugar. Junket and custards made with milk and eggs and water-packed fruits are preferable. Before the age of six months, many babies are unable to handle the roughage (fiber) in whole grains and therefore refined grains are usually preferred. As soon as he seems able to handle them, give him whole wheat and oatmeal and omit refined grains such as white bread and spaghetti. Whole wheat and oatmeal are preferable to rice, particularly white rice, because they have more protein.

What about packaged baby foods? Should you use them? Many nutritionists are beginning to question their value because they encourage mothers to wean children at too early an age. Many of these foods contain added salt and sugar to make the food more palatable to the parents. Extra salt in prepared baby foods may be a cause of hypertension in later life, although the case against it has not been proved. In the case of certain vegetables, however, packaged baby foods may be safer than home-prepared foods (see page 42). The packaged foods cost 2 to 3 times as much as comparable foods prepared at home.

A word about vitamins: some, such as thiamine, folic acid, and vitamin C, are easily destroyed by heat, so cook vegetables the minimum amount and wherever practical serve them raw. Infants under one may have a problem with raw vegetables, but raw fruits, such as ripe bananas, are usually agreeable to the child at six months or earlier.

## WEANING INFANTS ON LACTO-VEGETARIAN DIETS

The Seventh Day Adventists, who stress scientific nutrition, have had success in raising several generations of children on vegetarian diets that include milk and eggs. The Adventists have less disease in later life and live longer than people generally, although it's not evident to what extent diet is responsible for their good health.

Up to the age of six months your infant can get adequate nutrition from breast milk or formula, although an iron supplement is needed after the third month. By the end of twelve months, it's likely that the child will depend mostly on solid food. During the period of weaning, his nutrient requirements are extremely high: pound for pound, he needs more protein, more calcium, and more of most other nutrients than at any other time of life. As you can see from Appendix 1, a high-quality vegetarian diet that includes milk and eggs is adequate for infants in this age group. The only nutrient not supplied in adequate quantities is iron, so it's advisable to feed him an iron-fortified cereal or provide the iron in a supplement.

If you plan to bring up your child as a vegetarian, you'll want to accustom him to the types of food that should be the basis of a lifelong diet. In Chapter 2 we discussed the five basic food groups. With proper sieving and mashing, you can introduce your child to virtually all adult foods from these five groups by the end of his second year. He may reject some strong-tasting foods, such as broccoli, cauliflower, and cabbage, at six months, but then may take to them enthusiastically several months later.

## WEANING INFANTS ON VEGAN DIETS

The National Academy of Sciences, as we've seen, has given its blessing to vegan diets providing they include a variety of foods and are supplemented with vitamin B12. Neither the NAS nor any other official organization has provided guidance on the special problems of vegan infants. It's not surprising therefore that medical journals periodically report malnourishment among vegan children.

A vegan group that takes a sensible approach to infant feeding is the people at The Farm, the commune in Tennessee. Many of the original members had been lacto-vegetarians but others had followed fruitarian or macrobiotic diets. A sound nutritional program was started in the very early days (1971) but because of poor nutritional habits prior to coming to The Farm and the difficulty of getting everyone's agreement on a new approach to diet, some of the children were low on iron and vitamin B12.

A soybean milk dairy was set up. The soy milk was fortified with vitamin B12 and in the winter with vitamins A and D. Soy milk provides high-quality protein comparable to that of cow's milk. The children are also fed high-protein iron-fortified baby cereal, and if their blood tests show signs of anemia, they're given an additional iron supplement. Because of the high-protein quality of the soy milk and the baby cereal, the children get adequate protein.

According to the Tennessee Department of Public Health, this program has corrected the original nutritional deficiencies. Dr. J. O. Williams, Jr., one of the attending physicians at The Farm, says that nowadays everyone that he takes there comments on the robust good health of the children.

Vegan parents in England have also learned how to cope with the special requirements of early childhood. This is evident from a study done at Kingston Hospital by Dr. F. R. Ellis and Pamela Mumford, who examined sixteen children and adolescents ranging in age from one to eighteen. None of them had ever eaten animal food. Ellis and Mumford found them to be in good health and average in height and weight for their age. T. A. B. Sanders, another British nutritionist, studied thirteen lifetime vegan children and came to the same conclusion. Dr. J. O. Williams, Jr., who has examined vegan children at The Farm, has not tabulated data on their height but believes that they are as tall as nonvegan children of the same age. Parents may want to note, however, that no large-scale study has been conducted that might confirm whether children on well-balanced vegan diets grow to normal adult height.

The experience of vegans at The Farm and in England highlights the importance of soy milk in providing good-quality protein in the transition from breast-feeding to the largely solid-food diet of the younger children. Apparently, one of the major problems of malnourished vegan infants as reported in the medical journals was lack of such a source of easily assimilable protein during the critical period of weaning.

You can make soy milk at home but for infant feeding it is better to ask your pediatrician to recommend a commercial brand. The quality of commercial products is apt to be more uniform and they are ordinarily fortified with a variety of nutrients, including vitamin B12, vitamin D, calcium, iron, and riboflavin.

Vitamin B12, of course, is not ordinarily available in plant foods, so it's essential to have your child get it daily from fortified soy milk or some other source. Vitamin D is essential for proper calcium absorption, so it should be included in the soy milk, at least during the winter. During good weather, your infant ordinarily gets sufficient vitamin D from the ultraviolet rays of the sun acting on the skin.

Vegan diets, like other diets, supply less than the Recommended Dietary Allowances (RDA) of iron as set by the National Academy of Sciences for infants. However, the vegan diet exceeds the British allowance and the allowance set by the World Health Organization. Dr. F. R. Ellis notes that vegan infants in Britain have not displayed symptoms of iron deficiency. Commercial soy milk produced for infant use is fortified with iron, so there should be no question of a possible deficiency. Fortified soy milk also provides calcium and riboflavin. Green leafy vegetables supply adequate amounts of these two nutrients, so if your child is temporarily off these vegetables, he'll be covered by the soy milk.

The children at The Farm and also those studied by Ellis and Mumford get substantially less than the RDA for calcium, a mineral essential for proper bone growth. As Ellis and Mumford point out in their report on vegan children and adolescents, "many people achieve full stature and have good bones and teeth on similar low intakes provided that their diet contains adequate vitamin D." Apparently calcium and vitamin D, which promotes absorption of calcium in the small intestine, have been adequate for the children at The Farm, and those studied by Ellis and Mumford and Sanders have enjoyed normal growth. In some areas, including many parts of England where vegan children live, a substantial amount of calcium is supplied by ordinary tap water. Because you may not be able to count on getting much calcium from tap water in your area, it's wise to feed your children calcium-fortified soy milk.

Vegetables, particularly the dark green leafy type, are particularly important in infant vegan diets because they are by far the best natural source of calcium and also riboflavin, a vitamin potentially in short supply among vegans. They also contain substantial high-quality protein. As soon as you can after weaning, get your child accustomed to eating collards, kale, mustard greens, broccoli, lettuce (particularly the dark green types), and other high-nutrient vegetables, such as squash. Appendix 6 shows which vegetables are particularly nutritious.

Don't offer spinach, beet greens, or Swiss chard too often because they are high in oxalic acid, a substance that binds calcium, making it unavailable to the body. Spinach, carrots, and beets contain nitrate, a substance harmless in itself but which may be converted to nitrite after these vegetables are pureed at home. Excess nitrate may affect the infant's hemoglobin, causing a condition known as methemoglobinemia. Because of this, a group of experts on infant nutrition have warned that "the potential hazard of feeding infants spinach, carrots, or beets puréed in the home may outweigh any advantage of home preparation." Commercially prepared spinach, carrots, and beets apparently don't cause methemoglobinemia.

In addition to soy milk and high-nutrient vegetables you

should, of course, also include a variety of other vegetables, fruits, cereals, and nuts and seeds. Wherever practical, serve soy milk (or other bean products) at the same meal with either cereal or nuts and seeds, because these combinations improve the quality of the protein.

For infants who drink milk or eat meat, the order of introduction of solid foods is not too important. In the case of vegan babies, it is wise to introduce soy milk and high-nutrition vegetables first because of their need for calcium. After the age of one, the need for calcium actually declines for a while, and the child can get along well with fewer vegetables.

How do you know if your child is doing well? I put this question to Dr. Frey Ellis, who, in addition to being a consultant hematologist, is also president of the British Vegan Society. Dr. Ellis, who has probably examined more children on a strict vegan diet than any other physician in Great Britain, said, "Just notice their energy. If they're running about and have the energy of omnivore children, I wouldn't be at all worried about their diet. Obviously," he added, "if you found that they were becoming grossly underweight, you'd do something about it."

In recent years several articles in medical journals may have given the false impression that animal protein is essential for growth. One of these articles, which appeared in the *Journal of the American Medical Association* in 1974, carried the headline "Babies Who Eat No Animal Protein Fail To Grow at Normal Rate." The article reported that eight infants raised on a vegan diet tended to be underweight and got inadequate calories, protein, calcium, and riboflavin. In the opinion of Christine Trahms, the nutritionist who conducted the investigation, the infants appeared lethargic. Her conclusion: "The young child on the vegan diet containing no animal protein is at risk for growth." This conclusion is valid for the eight infants studied but it doesn't apply to all vegan infants, as the recent experience at The Farm and the studies of Ellis and Mumford and Sanders have shown. High-quality, easily assimilable protein *is* essential but this can be had from soy milk.

Many of the malnourished vegan infants reported on in the medical journals were apparently fed a macrobiotic diet. This particular variant of the vegan diet is, as we'll see in Chapter 9, often quite hazardous for infants and adults alike. The evidence from the English studies and the experience at The Farm in Tennessee show that *properly fed* vegan children are not at risk.

Although the evidence gives strong support to the safety of

balanced vegan diets for children, parents should be aware that no large-scale study has been made to check for possible long-term health disadvantages. For this reason, it is important that parents of vegan children explain the diet to their pediatrician. If the pediatrician strongly advises the addition of milk and eggs, it's wise to follow his or her advice.

# ABOUT BREAST-FEEDING AND THE INTRODUCTION OF SOLID FOODS

Until recently, almost all pediatric experts either favored or had a neutral opinion about prepared formula and the early introduction of solid food. These attitudes began to change particularly after publication of a 1972 study showing that the very early introduction of solid foods, together with bottle-feeding, tended to make children overweight and to provide them with much more protein than required. Excessive protein consumption early in life is a cause for concern because studies with animals have shown that, although it promotes speedy growth, it also shortens life.

Why should infants overeat when they are bottle-fed and weaned too early? No one is quite certain, but it may have something to do with the tendency for parents to coax the child into finishing the bottle. It may also be related to the sugar content of many solid foods, such as presweetened infant cereals.

Most authorities now agree that breast milk is the best food for babies, at least in the first weeks of life. It reduces the risk of gastrointestinal upsets, tetany, dehydration, allergy to cow's milk, and other hazards. Breast-feeding, besides being a comforting emotional experience for both mother and child, may also benefit the mother by using up fat in her body accumulated during pregnancy. Mothers who do not lactate may have a greater chance of being overweight in later life.

Dr. Malcolm Holliday, chairman of the Committee on Nutrition of the American Academy of Pediatrics, says that mothers should breast-feed their infants for six months. Other experts are not as specific on the time of weaning, but warn against the introduction of solid foods in the early weeks or even the early months of infancy. Many pediatricians suggest starting solid foods in the first six months because babies take to them more readily than when they're older and more opinionated. Some recommend solid food after the second month in order to provide sufficient iron, a nutrient that is virtually absent from breast milk. Solid food, however, can be delayed if an iron supplement is given. (Your pediatrician can advise on the type of iron supplement to give. He will probably also recommend supplements of vitamins A, C, and D.)

There is a problem with breast milk because it contains potentially toxic substances. According to testimony before the U.S. Senate Subcommittee on Health and Scientific Research, by Dr. William B. Weil, Jr., chairman of the Department of Human Development at Michigan State University, breast milk "may contain pathogenic bacteria and viruses, opiates, salicylates, barbiturates, antibiotics, lead, mercury, arsenic, and a host of fat-soluble chemical poisons." Neither Dr. Weil nor any other responsible authority claims to know what the long-term effects of these and other substances will be on the health of children.

Meat, fish, and poultry are the source of much of the foreign substances in breast milk and so vegetarian women are apt to have lower levels in their breast milk. Recently the Environmental Defense Fund and the federal government collaborated on a study of fifty women on a vegetarian diet. The study showed that they had one-third to one-half as many pesticides in their breast milk as did women on conventional diets. Their levels of polychlorinated biphenals, a highly suspect industrial contaminant, were close to those of the meat eaters.

The Environmental Defense Fund recommends eating low-fat dairy products such as skim milk and suggests avoiding butter, cream, ice cream, and high-fat cheeses. It also recommends corn oil margarine, as corn oil is less likely to contain pesticide residues than other oils.

Chemical contaminants are stored in fat deposits and so may take years to be eliminated. During breast-feeding, the mother draws on these fat deposits. Presumably, women who are long-time vegetarians would have fewer potentially toxic substances in their breast milk than more recent vegetarians.

Vegetables are not wholly free of toxic substances. You can, of course, reduce your consumption of these substances by eating vegetables grown without benefit of pesticides. Another way is to substitute frozen vegetables for fresh store-bought produce. Frozen vegetables are likely to be washed immediately after harvest and this eliminates most of the pesticides. Fresh produce is less likely to be washed and so the pesticides have time to penetrate more deeply into the plant, thus making home washing less effective.

# 4

## Vegetarian Diets
## from Preschool Years
## Through Adolescence

When vegetarian children are old enough to know that their diet is different, they'll begin to ask questions. How do you handle the problem? One mother said, "I let them know that they are in good company." Another parent said, "We don't make a big issue of it. If she wants to eat hamburger at school, it's up to her." Other vegetarian parents have a policy of serving their children meat at home if they demand it. Many vegetarian parents that I've talked to feel it's better to set a good example by their own eating habits and not make their children anxious or uncomfortable by bad-mouthing nonvegetarian foods.

A well-known leader of the vegetarian movement once said, "It's difficult enough for a child to be a vegetarian in this world, but it's very difficult to be a vegan." He believes that unless the child is brought up in a sheltered atmosphere, the discomfort of being different can be a problem and that vegan parents must be particularly adroit in handling the child's feelings.

How to be adroit is a question that I can't answer, but I'll pass on one nugget of advice from a vegan father: "Bring them up to think for themselves, and if they decide to drink milk or eat meat, don't complain."

## LACTO-VEGETARIAN DIETS

As your children get more teeth, they can eat a greater variety of foods. By the age of one most can eat raw vegetables, and by the age of two or so they can be eating much the same food as adults.

During the first year, your child normally triples his weight, but there's a marked slowdown in growth from age one until puberty. This explains why one-year-olds seem to lose their appetites, at least for a while. They may eat far less or far more than the officially recommended allowances. Don't let this bother you, because the allowances are averages. As nutritionist Jean Mayer once said, "Tables of allowances . . . are almost unusable as regards a particular child." The test of good health is not strict adherence to recommended intakes, but proper growth and energy. If your child fails to grow or is listless, then you should be concerned and take him or her to the doctor.

If you're worried about proper nutrition for your children, extra milk may not be the panacea. It's all too easy for parents, and particularly vegetarians, to overemphasize milk because dairy industry advertising and many nutritionists endlessly sing its praises. Generations of children have grown to maturity believing that milk, preferably in large quantities, is absolutely essential to health. Our "widespread milk-drinking neurosis," as one authoritative British textbook calls it, probably traces back to the views of Henry Sherman, one of the great pioneers in nutritional science earlier in the century, who believed that calcium was the nutrient most likely to be lacking in American and European diets.

Milk, of course, is a highly nutritious food, but there is a possible danger in overemphasizing it because of its saturated fat content. A good rule of thumb is to give children two cups a day up to the age of ten and three cups after that. Menus that include these amounts supply the large quantity of calcium suggested by the American RDA and exceed the British recommended intake by a wide margin. Also—and this is quite important—these amounts of milk supply the child's minimum requirement for vitamin B12. If your children insist on more milk, have skim or low-fat milk available. You may even be able to interest them in yogurt or cottage cheese as a milk substitute if you start them early enough.

To provide sufficient iron, feed your children beans and other iron-rich foods (see Appendix 6). If your child doesn't take to these foods, ask your physician whether an iron supplement is needed.

A group of nutritionists from the Loma Linda School of Health has recently published guidelines for vegetarian children. Every child is different and so the guidelines may not fit your child precisely. You may, however, find them useful for avoiding grossly unbalanced diets. Here, with slight modification, are the recommendations of the Loma Linda experts:

*Number of Servings*

|  | 1–3 Years | 4–6 Years | 7–12 Years |
|---|---|---|---|
| Milk and milk products | 2–3 cups | 2–3 cups | 3–4 cups |
| Vegetables—total* | ½–1 cup | 1–1½ cups | 1½–2 cups |
| (including green leafy) | (½ cup) | (½ cup) | (½ cup) |
| Vitamin C-rich fruit | 1 | 1 | 1 |
| (or juice) | (½ cup) | (½ cup) | (½ cup) |
| Bread and cereals† | 3 | 3–4 | 4–5 |
| Beans, cooked | ¼ cup | ½ cup | ¾ cup |
| Peanut butter | 1 tablespoon | 2 tablespoons | 3 tablespoons |
| (or nuts and seeds) | ½ tablespoon | 1 tablespoon | 1½ tablespoons |
| Eggs | 1 | 1 | 1 |
| Fats | 1–3 teaspoons | 2–3 teaspoons | 2–3 teaspoons |

* Amounts are in terms of cooked vegetables. For raw vegetables, double the number of cups.
† A serving is one slice of bread (preferably whole-grain) or ½ to ¾ cup cooked cereal.
Source: Based on I. B. Vyhmeister et al., "Safe vegetarian diets for children," *Pediat Clin N Amer* 24:203, 1977.

# VEGAN DIETS

Your child should get a variety of foods from the four basic groups: vegetables, fruits, grains, and beans-nuts. Keep soy milk on hand at all times. If necessary, flavor it with chocolate or pureed fruit. If obesity threatens, don't cut down on soy milk. Instead, cut down on nuts, seeds, and dried fruit. Some of these foods are good sources of iron, but cutting them out altogether should cause no problems except possibly for adolescent girls. Because their needs are particularly high, they may need an iron supplement.

Good-quality vegan menus based on the four food groups provide adequate amounts of other nutrients for children, including vitamin B12, which is supplied by fortified soy milk. Fortified soy milk also contains enough added calcium to satisfy the high requirement in the American Recommended Dietary Allowances.

The suggested servings of food for vegan children shown below are adopted with modification from the recommendations of the Loma Linda experts.

*Number of Servings*

|  | 1–3 Years | 4–6 Years | 7–12 Years |
|---|---|---|---|
| Fortified soy milk | 2–3 cups | 2–3 cups | 3–4 cups |
| Vegetables—total* | ½–1 cup | 1–1½ cups | 1½–2 cups |
| (including green leafy) | (½ cup) | (½ cup) | (½ cup) |
| Vitamin C-rich fruit | 1 | 1 | 1 |
| (or juice) | (½ cup) | (½ cup) | (½ cup) |
| Bread and cereals† | 4 | 4–5 | 5–6 |
| Beans, cooked | ½ cup | ¾ cup | 1 cup |
| Peanut butter | 1 tablespoon | 2 tablespoons | 3 tablespoons |
| (or nuts and seeds) | (½ tablespoon) | (1 tablespoon) | (1½ tablespoons) |
| Fats | 1–3 teaspoons | 2–3 teaspoons | 2–3 teaspoons |

* Amounts are in terms of cooked vegetables. For raw vegetables, double the number of cups.

† A serving is one slice of bread (preferably whole-grain) or ½ to ¾ cup cooked cereal.

Source: Based on I. B. Vyhmeister et al., "Safe vegetarian diets for children," *Pediat Clin N Amer* 24:203, 1977.

## MORE ABOUT FEEDING PROBLEMS

During infancy, you have complete control of the foods your child eats, but gradually you'll lose out to other influences—TV, neighborhood children, the school lunch program (it's often abominable), and coin machines filled with junk foods. You might as well use what influence you have in the earlier years to teach good dietary habits and hope that they'll carry over to adolescence, a period when your influence is likely to be at low ebb.

What can you do in these early years to help your child eat properly? First of all, don't have any rigid rules about feeding for they are resisted by the child and can create emotional stress. Stress may decrease appetite while actually increasing the need for some nutrients including protein and calcium.

Another thing that you can do is to provide the right atmosphere for proper eating. Keep your children in the habit of eating breakfast by eating it with them. Breakfast may not always be important for adults but it's wise to keep children in the habit because, as they grow older, there will be fewer and fewer opportunities to give them good food.

A third thing that you can do is to make vegetables tasty. Overcooking destroys flavor, while some vegetables, such as cabbage, develop a strong flavor when cooked too long. Try different methods of preparing vegetables, such as baking or frying. Some vegetables can be made much more appealing with the help of sauces. (See Chapter 13 for some useful sauce recipes.)

It is possible that some teenage girls, with their lower calorie needs and their frequent obsession with slimness, may not get enough calcium. In extreme cases there is the danger that girls who get inadequate calcium and vitamin D over an extended period will have stillborn or malformed children. It may take as long as six months for a girl with poor nutrition to build up her stores of calcium in preparation for pregnancy. For this reason it's wise for parents of a vegan girl to be sure she eats adequate amounts of calcium-rich vegetables and soy milk. If you find that she doesn't eat enough of these foods, give her calcium-fortified soy milk or switch her to cow's milk.

The late Haim Ginott, the psychologist from New York University, says: "Adolescence is a period of curative madness, in which every teenager has to remake his personality. He has to free himself from childhood ties with parents, establish new identifications with peers, and find his own identity." Freedom from parental ties often (usually?) includes complete rejection of nutritional advice. The best that you as a parent can do is to make wholesome foods always available and make them as tasty as possible. But beyond this, is there anything that you can do?

The answer is yes, if you're willing to be slightly calculating—and observant. Look for things that your teenager is concerned about and use these concerns, wherever practical, to encourage good nutrition. Two examples come to mind. If your teenage daughter is obsessed with slimness, point out to her the possible advantages of a vegan or largely vegan diet in weight reduction. It may not work, but if she eats more plant foods, including a variety of vegetables and fruits, she'll get better nutrition.

If she's concerned about acne, take her to a dermatologist. As part of the therapy, the doctor will probably advise a more wholesome diet. (Many experts believe that too much candy, cake, ice cream, and chocolate aggravates the ailment, although there is some dissent from this widely held opinion.) If your dermatologist knows anything about teenage nutrition, he'll recommend an improved diet. It wouldn't be unethical to remind him of his duty.

# 5

# Healthy Pregnancy on a Vegetarian Diet: The Special Requirements of Pregnancy and Lactation

A pregnant vegetarian has the same needs as a pregnant non-vegetarian. Both require well-balanced meals, both have to watch their weight carefully, and both have to get far more calories, vitamins, minerals, and particularly protein than before.

## LACTO-VEGETARIAN DIETS DURING PREGNANCY AND AFTERWARD

If you're a lacto-vegetarian you'll be choosing your extra foods primarily from the five basic groups: vegetables, fruits, grains, beans-nuts, and dairy products-eggs. If you do this, it's likely that you'll satisfy all the nutritional requirements of pregnancy except for iron and possibly folic acid. Your physician will probably recommend supplements of these two and, perhaps, other nutrients.

How much should you take from the five basic food groups? Here are suggested minimum servings that will provide all of the vitamins, minerals, and protein suggested in the recommended allowance, with the exception of iron. These recommendations apply to both pregnancy and lactation.

| | |
|---|---|
| Vegetables | 3 servings |
| Fruits | 3 servings |
| Grains* | 4 servings |
| Beans-nuts† | 2 servings |
| Dairy | 4 cups skim milk or yogurt |

These servings won't supply all of the calories that you'll need. The extra calorie requirement can be made up by fats, oils, desserts, or additional servings from the five basic groups. You will, of course, want to adjust your menu in order to maintain the weight gain advised by your physician.

Appendix 1 shows a typical day's menu. Menus similar to these have been used for several generations by the Seventh Day Adventists, one of the healthiest groups of people you'll find anywhere.

## VEGAN DIETS IN PREGNANCY AND AFTERWARD

In the early 1950s Drs. Mervyn Hardinge and Frederick Stare conducted a pioneering study on the health of vegetarians and vegans living in California. They found that all women who were normally on a vegan diet added milk and eggs during pregnancy. More recently, Dr. Frey Ellis and several of his British colleagues made a study of fourteen pregnant vegans, comparing them with eighteen pregnant women on omnivore diets. The vegans had averaged six years on their diet before becoming pregnant. Dr.

* A serving is 2 slices of bread, 1 cup of rice (cooked) or hot breakfast cereal, 2 ounces of ready-to-eat breakfast cereal, or ⅔ cup of spaghetti (cooked).
†A serving is 1 cup of beans (cooked) or 2 ounces of nuts (= 4 tablespoons nut butter).

Ellis found no significant differences between the two groups in terms of stillbirths, miscarriages, anemia, or toxemias of pregnancy. Six of the fourteen vegan women admitted to having occasional small amounts of milk during pregnancy.

The numbers in this study are rather small but that's not the case at The Farm, which has a policy of accepting pregnant women from outside the commune if they agree to come at least six weeks before the baby is born and to follow The Farm diet. They are also asked to go on a lacto-vegetarian diet before arriving at The Farm. Altogether, there have been well over 800 babies delivered there, half of them born to women from the outside. In the very early days, before their nutrition program was fully in effect, some expectant mothers at The Farm got inadequate protein, vitamin B12, and iron.

Nowadays all pregnant women at The Farm drink vitamin-fortified soy milk, eat lots of other soy products, and take prenatal vitamins and an iron supplement. During the last half of pregnancy, they are also given a calcium supplement. Signs of ill health due to poor nutrition are now unknown, according to Margaret Nofziger, The Farm nutritionist.

If you feel it's easier or safer to include milk and eggs, you should do so. There is little point in sticking to vegan principles if you feel anxious about your own health or the health of your unborn child.

There is one quite interesting fact about mothers who eat no animal foods. Dr. T. A. B. Sanders, one of the British experts on vegan nutrition, found that their breast milk had far more polyunsaturated fat and far less saturated fat than the milk of women who ate meat. The ratio of polyunsaturated to saturated fat in the diet strongly affects the level and type of cholesterol in the blood and so may be involved in the initiation and growth of atherosclerotic plaques, a process which many researchers now believe starts in infancy. Whether the radically different fat composition of vegan breast milk has a beneficial effect on infants we do not know. There is no evidence that it does any harm.

In Chapter 2 we discussed the four basic vegan food groups: vegetables, fruits, cereals, and beans-nuts. If you have been eating the minimum amounts from these four groups, you'll need to concentrate on getting considerably more protein, as this is the most critical nutrient for vegans during pregnancy. Most of your extra protein should come from soy milk since this is your richest source. You'll also need more calcium, and the best way to get this is by adding green leafy vegetables and calcium-fortified soy milk. Typical diet plans for pregnant and lactating women include these minimum amounts:

| | |
|---|---|
| Vegetables | 4 servings |
| Fruits | 2 servings |
| Grains* | 5 servings |
| Beans-nuts† | 2 servings |
| Soy milk | 4 cups fortified soy milk |

These diets provide more than 85 grams of protein, more than the U.S. Recommended Dietary Allowance, the British Recommended Intake, or the World Health Organization allowance. It's important to note that the suggested amounts apply to women of average size. Average is defined as 128 pounds before pregnancy, height of 5 feet, 4 inches, and medium frame. If you differ substantially from the average, your physician may recommend changes in the number of servings suggested above.

If you follow these suggestions for recommended amounts from the four basic groups, you'll probably have to cut down on the amount of fats, oils, and sweets that you usually eat. As for alcoholic drinks, there's virtually no room in the diet. This is just as well because alcohol can damage the fetus.

You will, of course, need a good source of vitamin B12. Unless you get it from fortified soy milk or other fortified foods, it's advisable to take a supplement. Dr. Sanders, one of the English experts on vegan diets, warns that if the pregnant mother's supply of vitamin B12 is marginal, the development of her child might be impaired. His warning is vividly illustrated by a case reported in the *New England Journal of Medicine* in which a six-month-old breast-fed infant born to a vegan mother suffered from severe megaloblastic anemia, dysfunction of the central nervous system, and coma. The mother had neither eaten animal foods nor taken a B12 supplement for eight years.

You should be under the care of a physician during pregnancy. If he is not familiar with the vegan diet, you may want to show him this book. He may want to modify the diet suggested here to suit your individual circumstances and he may decide that it is

*A serving is 2 slices of bread, 1 cup of rice (cooked) or hot breakfast cereal, 2 ounces of ready-to-eat breakfast cereal, or ⅔ cup of spaghetti (cooked).
† A serving is 1 cup of beans (cooked) or 2 ounces of nuts ( = 4 tablespoons nut butter).

wise to supplement your diet with iron, vitamin D, calcium, and possibly milk and eggs.

## CLEARING UP
## SOME MISUNDERSTANDINGS

During pregnancy, you'll experience many novel sensations. It's unlikely that any of these will be due to a vegetarian diet. Morning sickness, which occurs in the early weeks of pregnancy, is not related to food, although the symptoms can sometimes be relieved by having a light breakfast before arising. Heartburn and indigestion, which can be particularly troublesome in the last third of pregnancy, can be caused by pressure of the enlarged uterus on the stomach. For this condition, your physician will probably advise you to take frequent small meals, to avoid bending or lying flat, and to eat a bland diet.

If you have a symptom and suspect that it's related to vegetarian diet, discuss it with your physician. It's likely that he'll be able to resolve the problem without the need for you to abandon vegetarian principles.

# 6

## Older Vegetarians:
## Vegetarian Diets
## in Middle Age and Beyond

At the age of seventy-five you may weigh exactly as much as you did when thirty, but in the normal process of aging your body composition will change profoundly. You'll lose considerable bone and muscle and you'll gain considerable fat. It's the bone and muscle that require the calories and so your need for energy gradually declines. According to the averages, if you're forty-five, you'll need 5 percent less food than at thirty. At fifty-five, you'll need 10 percent less; at sixty-five, 20 percent less; and at seventy-five, 30 percent less.

Although your energy requirements decline, your need for virtually all other nutrients remains the same. Some authorities believe that the elderly may need more nutrients because they are under greater stress than the young. It's as if nature has set up a squeeze play that forces you to get more from less. How do you, as a vegetarian, handle this problem?

# DEALING WITH NATURE'S SQUEEZE PLAY

You can deal with the squeeze play by a combination of exercise and high-nutrition eating.

In Appendix 1, you'll find an example of high-nutrition vegetarian and vegan menus for people over fifty. These menus—or something like them, tailored to your individual needs—can help you maintain your ideal weight into your seventies and eighties. The best guide to keeping proper weight is, of course, a good bathroom scale, for no menu plan can take into account your particular frame size and level of activity.

The high quality of these diets is made possible by giving much more emphasis to nutrient-rich foods. Calorie for calorie, certain types of foods, including low-fat dairy products, most vegetables, and beans, have considerably more vitamins, minerals, and protein than others. The menus for those over fifty shown in Appendix 1 emphasize these foods, while still including substantial quantities of fruit and cereal. Most of the reduction in calories as compared to diets for younger people can come from reducing the consumption of butter, margarine, salad oil, and fattening desserts.

The menus satisfy the U.S. Recommended Dietary Allowance for all known nutrients. In the case of vegans, the RDA for vitamin B12 and calcium is met by using fortified soy milk. If you use soy milk that is not fortified with calcium, you may get less than the U.S. RDA of 800 milligrams, but you'll easily exceed the WHO recommended intake of 400 to 500 milligrams and the British Recommended Intake of 500 milligrams. Most experts feel that 400 to 500 milligrams is adequate but there are those, such as Dr. Leo Lutwak, who disagree. Dr. Lutwak, who is professor of medicine at the Los Angeles School of Medicine, believes that insufficient calcium leads to periodontal disease, the chief cause of tooth loss, and of osteoporosis (increased porosity of the bones). Dr. Lutwak suggests that everyone get 1000 milligrams of calcium a day in order to prevent these diseases.

Osteoporosis is one of the chief ailments of the elderly, particularly women. After the age of forty or so the skeleton begins to shrink and in four decades the loss may be as much as 50 percent. Among the symptoms are pain in the back and deformity of the spine which often takes the form of a hunchbacklike formation called "widow's hump." Although proponents of the calcium-deficiency theory have gained some acceptance of their view in recent years, the majority of medical researchers feel that no one yet has a satisfactory explanation of the cause of osteoporosis.

Recent studies by a group from Leeds, England, suggest that the proper therapy for women who are losing bone mass is administration of estrogen. As a possible alternative to estrogen (which might be contraindicated in some cases due to heart disease or other conditions), they suggest higher calcium intake.

If you are at all concerned about calcium, drink extra skim milk, eat extra greens, or substitute fortified soy milk for the unfortified type. Absorption of calcium tends to fall with age, possibly due to vitamin D deficiency, so be sure to get this vitamin either from sunlight or from a supplement.

It may also help if you avoid eating too much of those processed foods that contain added phosphorus. A low ratio of calcium to phosphorus may promote osteoporosis. Most common foods—the chief exception is green leafy vegetables—supply more phosphorus than calcium. Many processed foods contain phosphorus compounds used as emulsifiers or texturizers. Among the more common foods in which you'll find phosphorus compounds are:

| | |
|---|---|
| soft drinks | self-rising flour |
| evaporated milk | canned tomatoes |
| ice cream | candy |
| ice milk | sauces and toppings |
| chocolate syrup | pasta products |
| breakfast cereals | many baked goods |
| package puddings | cake mixes |

The manufacturers of some products, including baked goods, are not required by law to list the ingredients on the label. "Dough conditioners," which are listed on some baked goods labels, may contain a phosphorus compound.

Another factor which some researchers have implicated in osteoporosis is excessive acid consumption, particularly in the form of high-protein diets. According to the hypothesis, bone dissolves in an effort to buffer the excess acid from a high-protein diet. If the hypothesis is correct, meat eaters would be more apt than vegetarians to lose bone with increasing age. Dr. Frey Ellis and his colleagues in Britain attempted to compare osteoporosis in lacto-vegetarians and omnivores. Their study revealed no significant difference between the two groups, although there was some tentative indication that vegetarian females under sixty-five may suffer less from the disease than omnivore females.

A disease sometimes associated with osteoporosis is osteomalacia (softening of the bones). Older people who don't get vitamin D from food or from sunshine are likely to develop this disease. If you don't drink vitamin D-fortified milk or soy milk, your physician may recommend a supplement, particularly during the winter months.

You may have wondered whether nature's nutritional squeeze play—the continuing need for nutrients as we grow older and the lower need for calories—can be avoided by taking vitamin and mineral supplements. It's better whenever practical to depend on food for your nutrients. Food contains trace elements not supplied by supplements and also supplies fiber, which has a beneficial mild laxative effect. If you're a vegan, you will, of course, need a vitamin B12 supplement or a food fortified with B12. In some cases, your physician may recommend supplements of iron and vitamin D. It's better not to make a decision on iron and vitamin D yourself, as there could be unwanted side effects in certain cases.

Extra nutrients could be supplied by such "superfoods" as wheat germ and brewer's yeast. There is a problem with these foods, however. Both of them, and particularly brewer's yeast, are very high in phosphorus and relatively low in calcium. Fortunately, some nutritional yeasts contain more calcium than phosphorus (see Chapter 10).

## STARTING ON A VEGETARIAN DIET LATE IN LIFE

If you are a meat eater, can you expect any benefits by changing to a vegetarian diet late in life? It is highly probable that any diet which helps to keep you trim will be beneficial. If the vegetarian diet helps you to overcome nutritional deficiencies, you'll benefit. Anthony Albanese, who is Director of Nutrition and Metabolic Research of the Burke Rehabilitation Center in White Plains, New York, puts it this way: "Good nutrition appears to work on the favorable side of longevity, even though a few years remain."

In the opinion of some experts, atherosclerosis might be reversed by reducing the amount of saturated fat in the diet. Many people find it easier on a vegetarian diet to control their consumption of saturated fat, particularly if they don't substitute large amounts of cheese for meat. A vegetarian diet, because of its high fiber content, may also be helpful in relieving constipation.

# 7

## Vegetarian Athletes

Can vegetarian athletes really compete successfully against meat eaters? How can they get enough protein without steak? What is the best diet for vegetarian athletes?

There is no doubt that vegetarians can compete successfully against omnivores. Murray Rose, a vegetarian, was a triple gold medal winner in the 1956 Olympic swimming events. In the same year another vegetarian, William Pickering, swam the English Channel in record time. Alexander Anderson, an Australian vegetarian, is a record holder in weight lifting. Chip Oliver, a successful linebacker for the Oakland Raiders, claims that he played better after becoming a vegetarian. Peter Burwash, another vegetarian, has been the top-ranked tennis pro in both Canada (1971) and Hawaii (1973).

The most unusual vegetarian athletes in the world are the

Tarahumara Indians. The Tarahumaras, who live in the Sierra Madre Mountains of northern Mexico, play a game called raripuri in which competing teams of two or three players run almost continuously for 100 to 200 miles kicking a wooden ball about the size of a small grapefruit up and down the rugged mountain paths. Even at night the contest goes on by torchlight with the players stopping briefly every thirteen miles or so for a small amount of food and water.

The Tarahumaras rarely eat eggs, dairy products, or meat, but most of their calories come from corn and beans supplemented with potatoes, squash, pumpkin, chili peppers, citrus fruits, and other fruits and vegetables.

# WHAT ARE THE NUTRITIONAL REQUIREMENTS OF ATHLETES?

The misconception that athletes need large amounts of red meat is one of the most persistent of food myths. According to one account, the practice originated in Greece during the fifth century B.C. when two athletes who had been on the traditional, largely vegetarian diet ate large quantities of meat to increase their bulk and weight.

As an athlete you may sometimes need extra protein, but in all cases this can be supplied by vegetarian diets. The need for extra protein arises when muscles have to be built up during training. In certain contact sports such as hockey and football the tissues become so bruised that extra protein is needed for repair. During the teens, protein needs are relatively higher in relation to body weight than in maturity. If you are a teenage athlete training for a contact sport, it's possible that you may need somewhat more than the Recommended Dietary Allowance. Most authorities, however, believe that the RDA, which has a built-in cushion of 30 percent, to allow for individual circumstances, is adequate for most teenage athletes. The point is probably academic, for balanced vegetarian diets supply far more protein than the official allowance.

Athletes need the same nutrients as nonathletes except that they may require more calories. Sports with low energy needs such as golf, baseball, and the others listed in Table 4 ordinarily do not increase energy needs by much. If you're an adult and practice these sports less than an hour a day you can use the food guides in Chapter 2.

If you are a teenage athlete or need extra calories for endurance sports, it is wise to eat more of the basic foods. Here are recommended minimum servings:

| | |
|---|---|
| Vegetables | 4 servings |
| Fruit | 5 servings (may be taken as juice) |
| Grains* | 6 servings |
| Beans and nuts† | 2 servings |
| Dairy | 4 cups skim milk, yogurt, or fortified soy milk |

If you follow these recommendations, you'll get all of the protein, vitamins, and minerals that you'll need and about 2000 calories. Your extra calories can come from additional helpings of the basic foods, from fats and oils, and from desserts and snacks.

It may be important for young athletes to limit their fat consumption in order to help prevent atherosclerosis and other diseases in later life. The easiest way to do this is to avoid heavy use of high-fat snacks and desserts and instead emphasize those that are high in carbohydrates. (See Table 2, Chapter 2.)

Normal vegetarian diets for sedentary adults provide 60 to 90 grams of protein. For most athletes, this will be sufficient. Large additional amounts of protein may be counterproductive because they increase urinary excretion of calcium and so may inhibit bone growth. The addition of large amounts of calcium doesn't necessarily make up for the urinary loss. It is therefore wise, particularly for the growing athlete, to avoid protein supplements unless recommended by a physician.

How many calories should you eat? There are complicated formulas for computing the desirable amounts based on size and energy expenditure. Fortunately, calorie counting is not necessary for most athletes because weight control is almost automat-

---

*A serving is 2 slices of bread, 1 cup of rice (cooked) or hot breakfast cereal, 2 ounces of ready-to-eat breakfast cereal, or ⅔ cup spaghetti (cooked).
† A serving is 1 cup of beans (cooked) or 2 ounces of nuts ( = 4 tablespoons nut butter).

## TABLE 4
### Endurance Sports Requiring
### High Amounts of Calories

Football
Gymnastics (especially
  apparatus)
Handball
Hockey (ice and field)
Long-distance canoeing
Long-distance rowing
Long-distance running
Long-distance skating
Long-distance skiing

Long-distance swimming
Marathon running
Middle-distance running
Mountaineering
Pentathlon
Skin diving
Soccer
Water polo
Wrestling

### Sports of Short Duration
### or Less Intense Action Requiring
### Smaller Amounts of Calories

Archery
Baseball
Basketball
Boating (sailing and ice boating)
Bowling
Boxing
Canoeing, slow or moderate
  speed
Cycling, slow or moderate speed
Dancing
Diving
Equestrian sports
Fencing
Golf
Gymnastics
High jump
Hurdle races

Javelin throw
Judo
Pole vaulting
Rowing, slow or moderate speed
Shooting
Short-distance running
Short-distance skiing, slalom
Short-distance swimming
Shot put
Skating
Ski jumping
Softball
Sprints
Tennis
Volleyball
Weight lifting

Source: *Nutrition for Athletes* (Washington, D.C.: American Alliance for Health, Physical Education, and Recreation, 1971).

ic. If you are overweight, emphasize the basic foods rather than snacks or desserts. If you are underweight, you should get your nutrients from the basic vegetarian food groups but also include high-calorie, high-fat snacks and desserts. When you have reached normal weight, however, it's wise to de-emphasize the high-fat items. If you are a teenager and lose weight, it's wise to see a physician. Often such weight losses are due to a sudden spurt in growth combined with inadequate calories.

You may be plagued by flatulence from gas-forming foods such as beans, cabbage, onions, radishes, and cauliflower. Many vegetarians adjust to large amounts of beans, but if the problem persists try a different type of bean or try a processed form, such as texturized vegetable protein or bean curd (tofu). It also helps to chew foods thoroughly and avoid gulping too much air when eating. In Chapter 10, we'll discuss a cooking procedure that helps reduce the flatus-producing agent.

## PREGAME EATING

Many athletes have unpleasant symptoms before competition, such as bowel disorders  burping, abdominal cramps, and vomiting. Nervous tension is often the cause. Fortunately, there are certain measures which can relieve the symptoms. One of the most important of these is timing of the pregame meal. By eating about three hours before competition you allow enough time for digestion and yet not so long that hunger develops. Certain types of foods should be restricted at this meal:

- *Fatty foods* should be restricted because fat slows emptying of the stomach.
- *High-protein foods* should be restricted because they are a source of acids, which can only be eliminated by urinating.
- *Gas-forming foods* are obviously undesirable. Dried beans, cabbage, onions, radishes, cauliflower, and turnips have a reputation for causing belching and flatus, but if you are unaffected by these foods, they can be included in the pre-event meal.
- *High-fiber foods* create bulk and so can be a problem particularly in prolonged or intermittent sports.

Typical meals for vegetarians based on these restrictions are shown in Table 5.

---

For controlling bulk, here are some dos and don'ts to follow in the forty-eight hours before competition:

| Do Eat | Don't Eat |
|---|---|
| Cooked vegetables, potatoes, raw lettuce | Raw vegetables (except lettuce) |
| Raw oranges, bananas, and peeled apples, cooked fruit, fruit juices (except prune juice) | All other fruit, including tomatoes |
| Refined grains including enriched white bread and pasta | Whole grains, popcorn, beans |
| Skim milk, cheese Soy milk Eggs | Nuts, seeds, relishes, gravy |
| Sweeteners, including clear jellies | Jams, preserves |

Many athletes take candy or sugary drinks before competition to get a "quick energy lift." According to a study reported by Dr. David Costill, a leading expert on sports nutrition from Ball State University in Muncie, Indiana, the practice actually lowers performance in endurance sports. Sugar taken *during* prolonged exercise does not have this adverse effect but neither does it have a beneficial effect except perhaps in cases where the athlete has greatly lowered his blood sugar level after intensive exercise.

## HIGH-ENERGY SPORTS

In endurance sports such as football, long-distance running, or other high-energy sports listed in Table 4, the energy needs are quite high—4000 to 6000 calories as compared to about 3000 for many less active sports. Most sports in the low-energy group would be placed in the high-energy group if carried on intensively for several hours.

In sports where energy demands are low or of short duration you don't have to be too concerned with the source of your energy. In endurance sports, however, the source is important. To understand this, let's look at how energy is used and stored in the body.

The body utilizes energy only in the form of glucose, a carbohydrate which is a component of most foods, including common table sugar (sucrose). Glycogen, another carbohydrate, is the principal form in which the body stores energy for future conversion to glucose. Glycogen is stored in the muscles and in the liver. If your body stores of glycogen are built up, you are able to carry on sports activity longer. You can build up your glycogen stores by eating more carbohydrates. Most nonvegetarians get 40 to 45 percent of their calories as carbohydrates. Authorities on sports nutrition suggest that for long and hard training and conditioning 50 percent or more of your calories should be in this form. (The maximum proportion or amount of carbohydrates in your diet will depend on the type of activity.) Ordinarily, vegetarians do not have to make an adjustment to a higher level of carbohydrate for the proportion in their diet is usually about 55 to 60 percent.

Some athletes who engage in endurance sports employ a special technique variously described as *carbohydrate loading, glyco-*

TABLE 5
**Pregame Meals for Vegetarian Athletes**

| Lacto-Vegetarian | Vegan |
|---|---|
| *500-Calorie Meals* | |
| skim milk—1 cup | soy milk—1 cup |
| banana—1 large | banana—1 large |
| orange juice—8 ounces | orange juice—8 ounces |
| white bread—2 slices | white bread—2 slices |
| margarine—1 pat | margarine—1 pat |
| *900-Calorie Meals* | |
| skim milk—2 cups | soy milk—2 cups |
| banana—1 large | banana—1 large |
| mashed potatoes—1 cup | mashed potatoes—1 cup |
| white bread—2 slices | white bread—2 slices |
| margarine—1 pat | margarine—1 pat |
| apple juice—6 ounces | apple juice—6 ounces |
| canned peaches—2 halves | canned peaches—1 half |
| oatmeal cookies—2 | oatmeal cookies—2½ |

*Protein content of these meals is under 15 percent of calories, fat content less than 25 percent, and carbohydrate content over 60 percent.*

*gen packing*, or *muscle glycogen supercompensation*. Carbohydrate loading, by greatly increasing the glycogen stores in the muscles over normal levels, permits athletes to go a longer distance before exhaustion. The technique, as described by Dr. David Costill, involves two phases. In the first phase, the muscles are emptied of glycogen three or four days before competition by strenuous exercise. Then, for three or four days before the event, the athlete increases the proportion of carbohydrates to between 75 and 90 percent of total calories.* Dr. Costill feels that starchy foods such as pasta and bread are better suited to the process than sugary foods. Vegetarians, including vegans, should have no special problem in using the carbohydrate-loading technique.†

Carbohydrate loading is used only for endurance events that exceed thirty to sixty minutes. In shorter events, athletes draw to a much greater extent on their fat reserves for muscular energy and therefore don't benefit from the carbohydrate-loading technique.

# NUTRITIONAL SUPPLEMENTS FOR ATHLETES

Over the years there have been claims that nutritional supplements of one sort or another will improve athletic performance. Among these supplements are liquid protein, potassium and magnesium salts of aspartic acid, vitamin A, the B-complex, vitamin E, wheat germ oil, and gelatin. Normal athletic diets, including the vegetarian diets suggested in this chapter, supply all of the nutrients you'll need. There is no evidence whatsoever that any of these supplements will add to your performance.

---

* Another and older version of the carbohydrate-loading technique is similar to that described here but involves an additional three-day period in which a high-fat, high-protein, low-carbohydrate diet is consumed. This phase immediately precedes the high-carbohydrate phase. This version, which has been criticized by Dr. Costill and others as being no more efficient than the simpler two-phase process, has now found its way into some textbooks on sports nutrition.

† The carbohydrate-loading practice may be dangerous for some, particularly older athletes. In one case a forty-year-old long-distance runner with a high serum cholesterol level experienced cardiac pain and electrocardiogram abnormalities after carbohydrate loading. One authority, on the basis of this case, warns that "the effect of this practice on heart function is worrisome enough to caution all athletes against its use without expert advice from competent physicians."

# 8

## The Protein Myth:
## Adequate Protein Without Fuss

Did Germany lose the First World War because of bad advice about protein? This intriguing possibility is raised by the extraordinary case of Dr. Max Rubner. In 1914 he was a man of great influence in German scientific circles. He was also a strong proponent of the idea that protein promotes vigor and physical efficiency. In the words of an authoritative nutritional text:

> He probably did more than any army general to lose the war . . . for on his advice German agriculture was continued on the old policy of rearing large herds of cattle and sheep. No additional pastures were ploughed. His failure to realize that cereals can yield up to six times more dietary energy per acre than cattle contributed importantly to the defeats which followed in 1917. (Davidson et al., *Human Nutrition and Dietetics*, Sixth Edition [Edinburgh: Churchill Livingstone, 1975], p. 69.)

Overestimating protein needs has been a common failing in nutritional circles for almost a hundred years. In 1881, Carl Voit, a pioneer in nutritional science, suggested that 145 grams of protein a day was necessary. In 1941, the National Research Council, in the first edition of its Recommended Dietary Allowances, put the level for male adolescents at 100 grams. By 1973, in the eighth edition of the Recommended Dietary Allowances, the NRC recommended only 54 grams for this group.

No one in living memory has done more to perpetuate the high-protein myth than the late Adelle Davis. In her best-selling book, *Let's Eat Right To Keep Fit*, she claimed that ignorance of protein was the "greatest hindrance to good health." Sixty percent of affluent people in America get inadequate protein, according to her figures. "If you wish to maintain your attractiveness, vigor, and youthfulness as long as is humanly possible, it is probably wise to eat considerably more than the [National Research Council] requirements." Count your grams of protein carefully, she exhorts, an injunction that must have turned many of her faithful followers into nutritional accountants.

The mistaken emphasis on high-protein consumption by Adelle Davis and other health food writers such as Carlton Fredricks has undoubtedly contributed to some of the skepticism about the safety of vegetarian diets. I once asked a group of vegetarians and would-be vegetarians, "What's the most difficult nutrient to supply in a vegetarian diet?" Almost all of them said, "Protein." Their fears are unfounded. If you are on a reasonably well-balanced diet—either lacto-vegetarian or vegan—you need have no fear of getting inadequate protein. Even during the critical periods of growth, pregnancy, and lactation—periods when protein needs are highest—well-planned diets will provide enough.

## PROTEIN SIMPLIFIED

Why all the fuss about protein? Perhaps it goes back to the word itself, which comes from the Greek *prōteios*, meaning primary. And it is primary in at least one sense: you have more protein in your body than any other solid substance. About 44 percent of the solid material in the body of a normally lean man is protein. (Fat accounts for 36 percent, carbohydrates, 4 percent, and minerals, which are mostly in the bones, account for 16 percent.) Protein is found in every living organism from the smallest virus to the largest whale and is an essential component of every cell in the body.

Proteins are not only the chief building materials of most cells but also have many functions in regulation of body processes. Hemoglobin, an iron-bearing protein that is the chief constituent of red blood cells, is necessary for carrying oxygen to the tissues. Proteins help in maintaining the slightly alkaline reaction of the blood. Enzymes—catalysts for specific metabolic functions—are wholly or partly protein. Antibodies—substances that protect against bacteria and organic poisons—are made of protein. Many hormones—substances such as insulin and adrenaline that regulate certain body functions—are also protein in nature.

Proteins are composed of amino acids, which are complex molecules made up of nitrogen, carbon, oxygen, and, in some cases, sulphur. There are only twenty amino acids, but by varying the number and position of these an immensely large number of proteins can be manufactured. Of the twenty amino acids, the human body can synthesize all but eight: isoleucine, leucine, lysine, the sulphur-containing amino acids,* threonine, phenylalanine, tryptophan, and valine. In addition, histidine is needed by infants. These amino acids must be present in food and for maximum utilization they should be present in certain optimum proportions. The proportion of amino acids in eggs and milk is so close to the optimum that they are commonly taken as the standard against which other foods are measured. Eggs and milk are said to contain high-quality protein in contrast to some other foods, such as peanuts, which contain fairly low-quality protein.

## MEASURING PROTEIN

The measurement of protein can be a confusing subject. If you look at any standard nutrition table, you'll see that peanuts supply 119 grams of protein per pound, while a pound of milk (about one pint) supplies only 16 grams. The surprising fact is

---

* Methionine and cystine, the sulphur-containing amino acids, are usually grouped together because cystine can substitute for methionine to a large extent.

that milk is a far superior source of protein than peanuts. To understand why this is so, let us look at protein in a new way— grams per 100 calories. Peanuts have only 4.5 grams per 100 calories, as compared to 5.4 for milk. This is because peanuts are mostly fat, whereas milk has relatively little fat. When we take quality of the protein into account, the difference is even greater, because peanuts have a quality score of 43,* while milk has a score of 82. The amount of complete protein—total protein per 100 calories adjusted by the quality score—is about 1.9 grams for peanuts and about 4.4 grams for milk.

Let us take these figures one step further and express them in terms of protein calories per 100 total calories. Each gram of protein contains approximately four calories. On this basis, 100 calories of peanuts contain 7.6 calories of protein (4 × 1.9) while the comparable figure for milk is 17.6. To put it another way, 7.6 percent of the calories in peanut butter are in the form of usable protein as compared to 17.6 percent in the case of milk.

This type of measurement—the percent of complete protein in 100 calories—is shown for a variety of common vegetarian foods in Table 6. It provides a useful way of comparing the relative protein values of different food groups and of comparing them to safe minimum levels. The World Health Organization estimates that an adult should get at least 5 percent of his or her calories as complete protein. The safe minimum level for pregnant women and children under one, according to WHO, is 7 percent.

We can draw some useful conclusions from Table 6:
- Most of the basic vegetarian foods—fruits are the chief exception—are adequate sources of protein.
- Dairy products, soybeans, and green leafy vegetables are outstandingly good sources of protein. (But you would not want to depend too heavily on vegetables because of their bulk.)
- Beans and unrefined grains are better sources of protein than most nuts and seeds.

The table illustrates that vegans who get the bulk of their calories from vegetables, grains, and beans should have no problem in staying well above the safe minimum protein level as estimated by WHO. Lacto-vegetarians, with their reliance on dairy products, should have even less of a problem in getting

* The technical term for the quality score used here is *net protein utilization* (NPU). NPU takes into account not only the amino acid balance but also the digestibility of the protein.

## TABLE 6
### Percent of Complete Protein in Vegetarian Foods*

| | Dairy & Other | Grains | Beans | Nuts & Seeds | Vegetables† | Fruits |
|---|---|---|---|---|---|---|
| 50% | cottage cheese (38%)<br>skim milk (33%)<br>egg (30%)<br>brewer's yeast (28%) | | | | | |
| 25% | | | | | mushrooms (27%)<br>kale, spinach | |
| 20% | yogurt<br>Swiss cheese | | soybeans | | Swiss chard | |
| 15% | cheddar cheese<br>whole milk | | | | collards<br>mustard greens | |

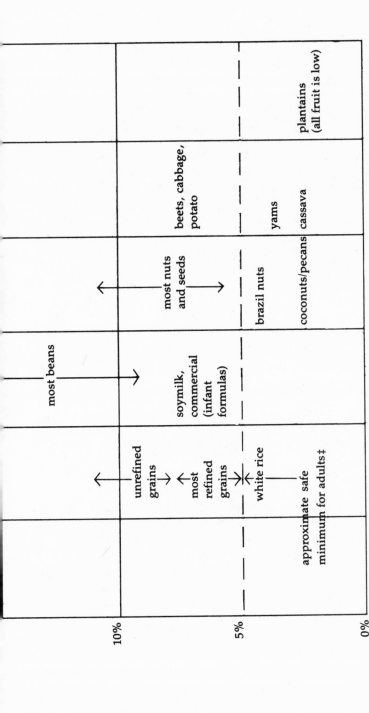

10%

most beans →

← unrefined grains →
← most refined grains →
soymilk, commercial (infant formulas)
← most nuts and seeds →

5%
← white rice →
approximate safe minimum for adults‡

brazil nuts
beets, cabbage, potato
yams

0%
coconuts/pecans   cassava
plantains (all fruit is low)

Source: calculated from Composition of Foods, United States Department of Agriculture Handbook No. 8 (Washington, 1963); Food Consumption Tables for Use in East Asia (Washington: United States Department of Health, Education and Welfare, 1972); and Amino Acid Content of Foods and Biological Data on Proteins (Rome: Food and Agriculture Organization of the United Nations, 1970). "Safe minimum" protein levels calculated from R. Passmore et al., Handbook of Human Nutritional Requirements (Geneva: World Health Organization, 1974).

* Complete protein is defined as total protein × net protein utilization, and is expressed in terms of protein calories as a percent of total calories in the food. Actual values may vary from indicated values due to variety, soil conditions, storage, processing, or other factors.

† Vegetables are not usually considered a major source of protein because of their bulk.

‡ The safe minimum for infants and pregnant women is 7 percent, and for lactating women, 6 percent.

adequate protein. Most of the people in developing countries who get inadequate protein depend excessively on foods like yams, cassava, and plantains (a type of tropical banana)—all of which are below the 5 percent minimum level set by WHO. As you look at Table 6, you'll see that white rice by itself supplies less than the theoretical safe level of 5 percent recommended by the World Health Organization. This means that if you depend entirely on white rice for your protein, you would, most likely, become protein deficient. Add a few beans and the protein value of the combination increases by up to 50 percent. This happens because the amino acids in the two foods complement each other. The rice is deficient in lysine but has a surplus of the sulphur amino acids, while the beans are deficient in the sulphur amino acids but have a surplus of lysine. Buddhist monks in Korea who eat an extremely large amount of white rice—60 percent of their calories—enjoy good health because they supplement their rice with beans and other nutritious foods. Many vegetarians in poorer countries are able to survive in good health with no animal food because they get quality protein from combinations of rice and beans or wheat and beans. Among other combinations that provide good protein value are beans and nuts or seeds, grains and milk, grains and egg, and brewer's yeast and grains.

Frances Moore Lappé in her best-selling book *Diet for a Small Planet* placed great emphasis on combining foods in the proper proportions in order to maximize protein values. For example, she provides recipes in which beans and rice are carefully balanced in the proportion of 1 to 2⅔. Vegetarians need not be concerned with such precision. By all means, eat complementary protein foods at the same meal, but let the proportions suit your palate. Even in pregnancy, when protein needs are highest, you can forget about the optimum proportions if you follow the recommendations in Chapter 5. As for children, there should be no problem if they get adequate amounts of cow's milk or soy milk with their meals.

The stress of everyday living may increase your need for protein but most such needs are taken into account by the official allowances. The American and Canadian standards for protein include a 30 percent cushion for normal day-to-day variation in need and also to allow for individual differences. The British include a 20 percent cushion in their allowance. If you are under severe physiological stress, such as in surgery, you may need extra protein, but in that case you will, of course, follow your physician's advice. In other situations, such as severe and sustained emotional stress, you won't really know whether you have a need for extra protein. At these times there's no harm in supplementing your usual supply with an extra glass or two of milk or soy milk.

There is no need for increased protein due to physical activity. You may need a small additional amount over the requirement for development of muscles during athletic conditioning. Profuse perspiring increases the need, but, because the body adjusts to sweat losses under prolonged heat conditions, the National Research Council does not make any special provision for this but assumes that the 30 percent safety margin in the RDA is an adequate cushion providing for possible protein losses due to sweating.

There is a danger of protein inadequacy if you cut calories drastically—say by 30 or 40 percent—as in weight-reducing diets. Teenagers who go on crash diets get so few calories that their protein may be used for energy instead of its normal body-building and repair functions. In this situation, a protein supplement is of little value for it, too, is apt to be used as energy. On crash diets, you are vulnerable not only to protein deficiency but to deficiency of other nutrients as well. You can avoid deficiencies by cutting down calories by a smaller amount—say 10 to 20 percent. The calories omitted should come mostly from fats and oils so as not to cause any deficiency in protein. If you give up two tablespoons of oil (or its equivalent in other fats) every day, it would mean a difference of 13 pounds over a six-month period.

The importance of avoiding a drastic cut in protein is underscored by recent work at the Massachusetts Institute of Technology. A research team from MIT headed by Neville Scrimshaw, probably the leading authority on protein deficiency, has questioned the generally accepted standards for protein. It claims that previous studies on which the allowances are based were technically inadequate, and on the basis of its own studies it suggests that the safe level, at least for adults, may be greater by 25 percent than the World Health Organization Allowances. This is of little practical significance for vegetarians except those on drastic weight-reduction diets. Even if the "safe minimum" in Table 6 has to be moved from the current 5 percent to, say, 6 or even 7 percent, vegetarians would have little trouble in meeting their requirements.

# 9

# A Pair of Unusual Diets

## MACROBIOTIC DIETS

George Ohsawa (1893–1966), the founder of macrobiotics, taught an extraordinary doctrine: The way to freedom and happiness lies primarily through proper diet. According to Ohsawa, macrobiotics is a practical and easy way for Westerners to attain *satori*, the sudden enlightenment that is the spiritual goal of Zen Buddhism. Macrobiotics is sometimes called Zen macrobiotics, but traditional practitioners of Zen disclaim any connection. Traditional Zen does not use diet as a means to satori.

The word macrobiotic is from the Greek *makro* (great) and *bios* (life) and so means "the great way of life." Macrobiotics is based on the concept of yin and yang, the principle that permeates all reality in traditional Chinese philosophy. Yin is feminine, passive, deep, dark, cold, and wet; yang is masculine, active, high, light, warm, and dry. Ohsawa classified foods according to whether they are yin or yang. Corn, sweet potatoes, oysters, pork, yogurt, pineapple, honey, and coffee are very yin. Buckwheat, onion, caviar, pheasant, goat milk, apples, safflower oil, and mu tea are very yang. Other foods fall in between these in a more or less continuous spectrum from yin to yang. Among all foods, brown rice is the most esteemed because it falls precisely in the middle of the spectrum. Enlightenment is attained by achieving a balance of yin and yang, so brown rice occupies a preeminent place in macrobiotic menus as a means of achieving balance.

As originally conceived by Ohsawa, the system is based on a hierarchy of ten increasingly restrictive diets ranging from −3, which includes cereal, fruit, vegetables, and animal foods, to the +7 diet, which consists of nothing but brown rice. Beginners are expected to start at the lowest level and work up quickly to at least the +3 level in which 60 percent of the food is whole-grain cereal, usually brown rice. The animal foods allowed include fish and dairy products but exclude meat and poultry. Most macrobiotics apparently are vegetarian. Those who adhere to the +3 level or higher are vegans.

Ohsawa believed that the +7 diet was a cure-all for a large variety of conditions, including apoplexy, arthritis, burns, cancer, diabetes, gonorrhea, heart disease, hemophilia, frigidity in women, insomnia, leprosy, paranoia, Parkinson's disease, schizophrenia, sterility, syphilis, and lesbianism.

The higher levels and particularly level +7 are dangerous if carried on for more than several days. At least one death is blamed on the macrobiotic diet and many cases of scurvy, anemia, and emaciation have been reported. Even among those who don't follow the extreme forms of the diet there can be problems. A study of people who were apparently on middle-level diets—50 to 70 percent cereal—showed that they were grossly deficient in several nutrients, including riboflavin and, among women, iron. Their most important deficiency was in calories: both men and women on the diet got less than half of the calories suggested by the RDA.

Ohsawa exhorted his followers to drink liquids sparingly. The adult body needs between 2 and 3 quarts a day for proper functioning. Some of this comes from the water in food, but food by itself doesn't normally supply all of the body's needs, so additional liquids are needed. When water is inadequate there is a tendency for kidney stones to form and kidneys may fail.

There is also a potential danger from a substance called phytic acid. This substance, which is found in unrefined cereals, including brown rice, binds minerals including calcium, iron, and zinc, and so makes them unavailable for absorption in the intestines (see Chapter 10). In ordinary vegetarian diets where whole grains are eaten in moderation, there is no apparent ill effect from phytic acid, but there is a possible danger if you eat very large amounts of whole grains over a period of months or years.

The greatest danger of a macrobiotic diet is not to adults but to newly weaned infants. As with adults, a major problem is getting sufficient calories. One fourteen-month infant got only one-third of the RDA for calories and was grossly deficient in at least six vitamins and minerals. The child had rickets, apparently as a result of extremely low calcium consumption. Macrobiotic children tend to be smaller than other children because of their poor diet.

Parents should be wary of using Kokoh, a macrobiotic infant food based on sesame seeds, brown rice, adzuki beans, and small amounts of wheat, oats, and soybeans. It is not clear whether this mixture provides adequate protein for newly weaned infants. A group of researchers from the University of Michigan who have studied the product say that "in the dilutions recommended and used, infants would have difficulty in meeting their energy requirements, and they face a real risk of protein deficiency."

## HOW TO GET ADEQUATE NUTRIENTS ON A MACROBIOTIC DIET

If you are on a macrobiotic diet, there are certain things that you can do to increase your chances of getting good nutrition:
- Get adequate calories—approximately the amounts recommended in Appendix 3.
- Choose foods that will give you enough of the essential nutrients. Use either Table 1 or 3 (Chapter 2) as your basic guide.
- Drink at least four glasses of water daily.
- Watch your sodium consumption. Use miso, gomasio, and tamari sparingly as these are very high in sodium.
- If you are eating little or no animal food, take a vitamin B12 supplement.

Don't wean infants on Kokoh. This supplies marginal protein value. Wean them instead on either milk or fortified soy milk. Keep your older children on the two lowest diets (−3 and −2)—no more than 20 percent cereals—and if you don't feed them milk, give them fortified soy milk.

During pregnancy and lactation it is also important to keep to the two lowest diets. Rely on skim milk or fortified soy milk—at least a quart daily—to get adequate protein and other nutrients.

Those who live in one of the centers of macrobiotic activity, such as Boston, San Francisco, or New York, seem to be aware that Ohsawa's advice shouldn't be taken too literally. For those outside the larger metropolitan centers, however, there is usually little guidance. There is, for example, no manual explaining the principles followed by the more skeptical disciples. Instead, you'll find older texts—usually in health food stores— that contain Ohsawa's less than trustworthy advice. Several of Ohsawa's followers have published equally unreliable works. It's wise to disregard completely the nutritional advice in any book written by Ohsawa or his disciples.

## ARE THERE ADVANTAGES TO MACROBIOTIC DIETS?

People who go on macrobiotic diets tend to lose weight and are rarely obese. Some may be underweight in comparison to ideal weight as given in standard height and weight tables. This is not necessarily a cause for concern if you get adequate nutrients.

A macrobiotic diet may help protect against atherosclerosis and high blood pressure. There's a recent study from Boston showing that macrobiotics have a lower blood cholesterol level and lower blood pressure than a matched group on a typical American diet.

Low weight, low serum cholesterol, and low blood pressure are not insignificant advantages. If you enjoy these advantages and avoid the common nutritional deficiencies of the macrobiotic diet, you'll be far healthier than the average American.

## FRUITARIAN DIETS

Most people who call themselves fruitarians live on raw fruits, vegetables, and nuts, and many also eat sprouted beans and sprouted grains. Those who adhere strictly to the diet never use fats, oils, sugar, salt, and other flavorings. Fruitarians are sometimes called raw food eaters.

They believe that their diet is the "natural food of man," to use the phrase of Hereward Carrington, an early twentieth-century fruitarian advocate. According to the theory, early humans and prehumans evolved on a diet of raw fruits, nuts, and foliage. Modern humans, by giving up this original diet, have brought on themselves the many diseases of civilization—heart attacks, strokes, hypertension, diabetes, cancer, and other major illnesses.

The fruitarians want to turn the nutritional clock back to a time that may never have existed, for it's not clear that our ancestors evolved on a diet such as they advocate. *Homo sapiens*, during most of his several hundred thousand years of existence, has been a hunter of big game, although plant foods account for more than half of his diet. Before *Homo sapiens*, there was *Homo erectus*, who was also probably a big-game hunter. Before him, we can trace man's ancestry to *Ramapithecus*, a subhuman who flourished six to fourteen million years ago. We know virtually nothing about his eating habits. Before *Ramapithecus*, there were many other primates, but paleontologists don't know which of these were our ancestors; nor do they know what these primates ate. Some might have been fruitarians, and it's just as likely that others, like modern apes in the wild state, ate insects, birds' eggs, and small animals in addition to their staples of fruit, nuts, and green foliage.

There is one part of the fruitarian argument that is historically correct: primitive humans, during most of the two million or so years of their evolutionary development, ate foods raw: the earliest use of fire goes back about four hundred thousand years or so. A certain amount of raw fruits and vegetables is desirable in any normal diet, but there is no proved advantage to eating everything raw.

We know very little about the health and longevity of early humans but it's probable that, like modern hunter-gatherers such as the !Kung bushman of Botswana, they didn't suffer from cardiovascular diseases, diabetes, and other ailments that afflict industrialized societies. Even if we assume that our far distant ancestors didn't suffer from these diseases, we couldn't attribute their health solely to diet.

One of the few scientific attempts to evaluate fruitarianism was made in the early 1970s by a group of researchers from the University of Pretoria in South Africa. The group, which was headed by Dr. B. J. Meyer, became interested in the diet after examining a woman who had eaten nothing but fruits and nuts for twelve years. The woman was in excellent health and enjoyed her strenuous routine as a physical education instructor. Dr. Meyer and his colleagues were intrigued by the case because there had been considerable discussion in the press about the adequacy of the fruitarian diet. They also wanted to investigate the possibility that the diet might protect against atherosclerosis.

In order to provide more information, they put twenty-seven adults—nine Bantus and eighteen Caucasians—on a fruitarian diet for twenty-four weeks. The diet included carrots and tomatoes. Every participant had to eat about two ounces of peanuts, cashews, or walnuts (for protein) and one-half to three-quarter pounds of avocados (for fat) each day. Fruit could be fresh, dried, or juice. Participants had to have at least 2400 calories daily and were allowed more in the form of fruit. This diet provided adequate nutrients. None of the participants suffered any ill effects, but ten out of the eighteen Caucasians ate other foods, apparently because their social and professional obligations made it awkward to stick to the test foods.

Dr. Meyer and his colleagues suggest that the diet may have health advantages. Those participants who had previously been overweight slimmed down to their ideal weight during the test. They had a tendency toward lower blood pressure, which could be due to weight loss and also the relatively low sodium content of the diet. Some of the participants also had reductions in serum cholesterol and triglyceride levels, possible signs of lower atherosclerosis risk.

## FRUITARIAN ATHLETES?

It is possible for trained athletes to run at least as well on a fruitarian as on a conventional omnivore diet. This was demonstrated by B. J. Meyer and his colleagues, who studied nine students between the ages of seventeen and twenty-four. The students were on a conventional omnivore diet for a year or more during which they exercised every day for an hour. They were then put on a high-protein diet for several weeks followed by a high-carbohydrate diet for a few days immediately prior to competition. In the competition they ran a medium-length course (for most of them the course was 8 kilometers).

Immediately after this, the students went on a fruitarian diet for fourteen days during which they got about two-thirds of their calories as carbohydrates. On the fourteenth day they ran over the same course and every one of the nine improved his or her performance. The improvement was not statistically significant but it suggests that the diet may have improved performance.

## THE SAFETY OF FRUITARIAN DIETS

Dr. Meyer's work shows that *over a twenty-four-week period* a fruit, nut, and vegetable diet of the type eaten by his test subjects is adequate for healthy adults. His study does not tell us what happens when you follow this diet over a longer period—five years, ten years, or a lifetime. Because the fruitarian diet is so restrictive, professional nutritionists do not recommend it.

It is unfortunate that the fruitarian diet hasn't had the benefit of additional scientific evaluation, for it's possible that the diet may have advantages for some people. It may, for example, be a good way for some to regulate their calorie consumption. As normally practiced, the diet doesn't include extra salt and so it may protect against hypertension.

It's possible that part-time fruitarianism—practiced when fruit is in season—would be good preventative medicine for those on typical Western diets for most of the year. We won't know whether the fruitarian diet has any such advantage unless medical researchers conduct long-term studies of its effect on health.

I don't advise you to go on a fruitarian diet for more than a few weeks unless you do it under a doctor's supervision. If you go on the diet there are several things you can do that will be beneficial:
- Eat a variety of nuts and seeds, but emphasize those that are better protein sources, such as pumpkin, squash, sunflower seeds, and peanuts.
- Stay at or close to the Recommended Dietary Allowance for calories.
- Take a vitamin B12 supplement.

One thing that you should definitely avoid is uncooked beans. Some fruitarians grind them up to make a paste. Beans *should never be eaten raw* because they contain toxic substances that are destroyed only by cooking. However, sprouted beans are not toxic.

Don't try a fruitarian diet during pregnancy. Theoretically, it is possible for the diet to supply all of the nutritional needs during pregnancy except vitamin B12, but to get these nutrients you would have to eat considerably more raw vegetables, nuts, and seeds than you're accustomed to. With 6 to 8 pounds of raw vegetables (chosen for good protein quality) and 5 to 8 ounces of nuts a day, you could get sufficient protein, the most difficult nutrient to supply in a fruitarian diet. You should be aware, however, that nutritionists know so little about this diet that they can't predict what problems you might have.

Don't put your children on a fruitarian diet. It would be difficult for them to get adequate protein and particularly calcium, and there is a big risk that they will not reach their full growth potential. For girls, the diet is unlikely to provide adequate buildup of nutrients for the stress of pregnancy.

## PURE FRUITARIANISM

Although a diet of fruits, nuts, and raw vegetables may seem freakish to ordinary vegetarians, there are some who want to go even further. A girl once told me, "I want to eat just fruit— nothing else. I want to give up nuts and vegetables and then I'll be an energy transformer and live up there."

H. Jay Dinshah, president of the North American Vegetarian Society, reports that in his travels through twenty-five countries he has yet to find anyone who has lived on a pure fruit diet for an extended period. The reason is apparent if you look at Table 6 (Chapter 8), which shows that fruit does not have enough protein to sustain life. Fruit lacks vitamin B12 and is generally deficient in several other nutrients, including zinc and folic acid. Even though the diet is a nutritional absurdity, reports that someone or other has spent years existing on fruit alone continue to circulate. Invariably, when you find someone who says, "Yes, I eat only fruit," it turns out that there's a problem of definition. In explaining himself, he might say, "I live on the fruit of the earth," and by this he means not only fruit as commonly defined, but also nuts and vegetables. The claims for complete fruitarianism can be misleading and possibly even dangerous for anyone who isn't aware of the semantic confusions.

# PART TWO

# VEGETARIAN
# FOODS and RECIPES

# 10

## A Close Look
## at Vegetarian Foods—
## and Vegetarian Food Myths

### VEGETABLES

Some natural food proponents look down their noses at frozen vegetables. It's true that the best tasting, most nutritious vegetables are usually fresh picked from your own garden, but if you can't get fresh picked your best alternative may be frozen vegetables. "Fresh" produce from the store may be several weeks old by the time it reaches your dinner table. It's often wilted and has lost much of its nutrient value. The freezing process preserves most of the nutrients and much of the original taste because freezing is done shortly after picking. There are exceptions in the case of some frozen vegetables so if a particular nutrient, say, iron or calcium, is important to you, it's wise to check the nutritional contents on the label. The biggest problem with frozen vegetables is the defreezing and refreezing that often occurs during distribution. This cuts nutrient value and alters flavor. If you buy frozen vegetables in plastic bags, look for those that are loose. If they are clumped, this indicates that defreezing and refreezing has occurred. Canned vegetables usually have less nutrient value than frozen.

As a group, common vegetables have more nutrients—calorie for calorie—than other natural foods. Among vegetables there are big variations in nutrient value, and it's important to know about these. There are four nutrients in particular that should be of interest—vitamin A, iron, calcium, and riboflavin. All vegetarians will want to include a good source of vitamin A in their diets and for this the green and yellow vegetables are an outstanding source. Women, who are sometimes deficient in iron, may want to eat some of the iron-rich items, such as spinach and mustard greens. Vegans may want to emphasize vegetables that are rich in calcium and riboflavin, two nutrients that are not available in quantity from other natural plant foods. Appendix 6 shows key nutrients in common vegetarian foods.

Don't use Appendix 6 as a guide for excluding vegetables. Potatoes, for example, are not particularly high in most nutrients, but they are an excellent source of energy, niacin, and fiber, and provide a certain amount of protein. Others, such as eggplant and cauliflower, although comparatively low in nutrients, are invaluable in making tasty vegetarian dishes. Raw vegetables commonly used in salads may not supply many nutrients individually, but when you put them together in a large salad their nutrient contribution is substantial.

## FRUITS

Fruits, and particularly citrus fruits, are good sources of vitamin C. A few—apricots, peaches, and watermelon—supply vitamin A activity. Dried fruits contain substantial amounts of iron. Fruits have small amounts of the B-complex and minerals, but if you eat a lot the total contribution of these nutrients is substantial.

Fruits are bulky foods—they contain much fiber—and so they're apt to have a mild laxative effect. If you take fruit juice rather than the whole fruit, you miss out on the laxative benefit and on whatever other benefits the fiber may confer.

# CEREALS

Whole-grain cereals are those which contain all three edible parts of the seed: the germ (rich in vitamins); the bran (rich in minerals and fiber); and the endosperm (mostly carbohydrate). Refined cereals, such as white flour, are mostly endosperm.

Table 7 shows the principal whole-grain and refined products. Also shown are those products which are intermediate in nutritive value between whole grains and the highly refined cereals.

Whole grains are good sources of fiber and fairly good sources of the B-complex and of minerals. Most refined cereals are enriched with thiamine, riboflavin, and niacin, but usually not with other nutrients lost in the refining process.

Over the years there has been discussion of the possible adverse effects of a substance called *phytic acid*, which is present in large amounts in whole-grain cereals. Phytic acid binds with calcium, iron, zinc, and other minerals, making them unavailable to the body. Fortunately, the digestive juices apparently develop the ability over time to separate the minerals from the phytic acid. Some cereals, including rye and wheat, contain the enzyme phytase, which breaks down the bound minerals. The phytase is activated when bread is leavened with yeast. In certain parts of the Middle East, where very large amounts of unleavened bread are eaten, children have suffered from delayed sexual development due to insufficient zinc. Their bread contained considerable zinc but was bound by the phytic acid. Indian children living in Britain may have developed rickets in part because of low absorption of calcium from unleavened bread.

Apparently, phytic acid is not a threat except to those who eat excessive amounts of whole grains. Those on a macrobiotic diet, in which 50 percent or more of calories are in whole grains, may be at risk. The adverse effects reported thus far have been primarily to children and teenagers, so it's wise not to feed them too much unleavened bread.

# BEANS

Beans, peas, and lentils—the legumes—have the ability through their root tubercles to absorb nitrogen from the air with the aid of bacteria in the soil. The nitrogen is the basis for their

| | | | | | | |
|---|---|---|---|---|---|---|
| | | **TABLE 7** | | | | |
| | | **Classification of Cereal Products by Nutritive Value** | | | | |
| *Nutritive Value* | *Wheat* | *Rye* | *Rice* | *Corn* | *Oats* | *Other* |
| *High* (whole-grain or mostly whole-grain) | wheat berries<br><br>whole wheat flour<br><br>whole wheat bread<br><br>wheat breakfast cereal, hot<br><br>shredded wheat | whole rye grain<br><br>rye flour, dark<br><br>rye wafers | brown rice | fresh, on cob<br><br>frozen | rolled oats (including both regular and quick) | millet<br><br>buckwheat flour, dark |
| *Intermediate* | bulgar (parboiled wheat)<br><br>cracked wheat bread | pumpernickel bread<br>rye flour, medium<br><br>rye bread, American style | converted rice | cornmeal, unbolted | | |
| *Low* (highly refined) | white flour<br><br>pastry flour<br><br>farina<br><br>all expanded breakfast cereals<br><br>most flaked breakfast cereals | rye flour, light | white rice<br><br>instant rice | corn flour<br><br>cornmeal, degermed<br><br>corn grits<br><br>hominy | | buckwheat flour, light |

high-protein content. Mature legumes—they are usually dried—have more protein than immature legumes, such as garden peas.

Beans help lower serum cholesterol, a fact which was noted many years ago by Ancel Keys. Keys, who is one of the leading experts on fat metabolism, wondered why the bean-loving Neopolitans had a lower cholesterol level and less coronary disease than Americans. After studying the diet of the Neopolitans, he developed the hypothesis that the complex carbohydrate in beans was the beneficial agent. To test this hypothesis, he conducted an experiment in which twenty-four men ate about 6 ounces of beans a day. Their cholesterol level was 9 percent lower than when they ate a control diet. In the control diet, the beans were replaced by bean protein and simple carbohydrate (sugar). Other studies have confirmed Keys' findings. Beans by themselves don't lower cholesterol levels by all that much, but if you use them as a substitute for fatty meat or high-fat dairy products you may be able to lower your serum cholesterol level substantially.

Soybeans are among the most valuable of vegetarian foods, not only because of their high-quality protein but because they can be made into soy milk and tofu (soybean curd). Tofu has a soft texture and, unlike soybeans, has a delicate flavor. Sometimes called soy cheese, it is high in protein and low in fat and is used in a variety of recipes, including casseroles. Two other soy products that are widely used in the United States are soy sauce and miso (soybean paste). These products are very high in sodium. Some medical researchers believe that the sodium in these foods contributes to the large number of strokes among the Japanese.

Beans contain toxic substances, including hemagglutinins (which clump red blood cells, causing goiter) and trypsin inhibitors (which retard growth), but these substances can be eliminated in normal cooking. It is not advisable, as some people do, to grind up raw beans and use the powder uncooked.

Beans cause flatulence but the body tends to adjust to this over time. You can reduce it further by soaking the beans prior to cooking and then discarding the soaking water. This helps remove the oligosaccharides, complex sugars which contribute to flatulence. In recent years the flatus-causing activity in some varieties of beans has been reduced. If one type causes you a problem, try another type. Thorough chewing also helps to reduce flatulence.

| | | TABLE 8 | |
| :--- | :--- | :---: | :--- |
| | | **Preparation of Beans** | |
| | *Soaking* | *Regular Cooking* | *Pressure-Cooking* |
| Beans, soy-beans, whole peas | Add salt, boil for 2 minutes, soak for 1 hour or overnight in 6–8 cups water to every pound of beans. Overnight soaking in warm room without prior 2-minute boil may result in sourness. | Drain soak water, add 6 cups hot water (1 inch above beans). Cooking time depends on locality where grown, age of beans, hardness of cooking water, and whether beans have been prepro-cessed to cut down cooking time. Soy-beans take longest to cook. Black, brown, red, kid-ney, and Great Northern beans, whole peas, and chick peas (gar-banzos) take less time. Pink, pinto, lima, and navy (pea) beans take still less time. The least time is needed for lentils, split peas, and black-eyed peas. | All types except split peas can be pressure-cooked. Fill pressure cooker no more than ⅓ full with beans and wa-ter. Add teaspoon or 2 of oil to prevent foaming. Esti-mated cooking times given in cookbooks are often too high, so it's better when ex-perimenting to undercook. For soybeans try 20 minutes; for black, brown, red, kid-ney, Great North-erns, whole peas, and chick peas, try 10 minutes. For pink, pinto, limas, and navy beans try 8 minutes. For len-tils and black-eyed peas, try 5 minutes. If beans are too hard you can cook further. |
| Split peas, except for soup | Add salt, boil for 2 minutes, soak for ½ hour in 6–8 cups of water for every pound of peas. | | |
| Split peas for soup, lentils, black-eyed peas | No soaking re-quired. | | |

If you do a lot of bean cooking, get a pressure cooker. It will save you considerably in fuel costs and cooking time. The most practical type is the 6-quart size that cooks at 15 pounds pressure. Cast aluminum is preferable to steel because it distributes the heat more evenly. Pressure cookers are completely safe as long as you follow the instructions supplied by the manufacturer.

When buying mature beans, look for those with bright color, uniform size, and no cracks. Beans that lack color are not fresh and will take longer to cook, although taste may not be affected. Lack of uniform size results in uneven cooking with the smaller beans being overcooked or the larger ones undercooked. Dry beans store well for several months in tightly covered containers kept in a dry, cool place (50 to 70° F.). Mixing of new with old beans results in uneven cooking.

As a general rule, 1 cup of dried beans yields 2½ cups of cooked beans. Some beans are preprocessed and require no soaking. If you buy in bulk or from a bulk container, there are unlikely to be directions for soaking and cooking, in which case use the preparation instructions from Table 8.


## NUTS AND SEEDS

Nuts and seeds can become infected with aflatoxins, substances suspected of being a chief cause of liver cancer. These toxins are produced by the mold *Aspergillus flavus*, which grows on a variety of plants under moist conditions and most notably on peanuts. Growth of the mold occurs when peanuts are stored above 70 percent relative humidity and when the nuts are damaged in harvesting and by insects. The best safeguard against contamination is adherence to proper storage conditions, and thorough government inspection. Roasting reduces the level of aflatoxins, but leaves residues in amounts which may still be toxic.

Liver cancer is not a major problem in America, thanks in part to fairly stringent standards enforced by the Food and Drug Administration. (In parts of Africa, where drying procedures are ineffective, liver cancer is a major cause of death.) According to FDA standards, lots with more than 20 ppb (parts per billion) cannot be used as human food. In the view of several experts, this is not a safe standard because aflatoxin B, the most potent form, has produced liver tumors in rats fed only 15 ppb for less than a year and a half. The British medical journal *Lancet* recommended in an editorial that a goal of 0.1 ppb be set, as this level has no apparent effect.

Vegetarians who depend to a great extent on peanuts and other nuts may be particularly at risk from aflatoxins. Until the FDA changes its standards, the best procedure short of giving up peanuts is to eat them roasted and to keep switching brands in order to avoid one that may be particularly high in aflatoxins.

## DAIRY PRODUCTS

Cup for cup, skim milk and low-fat milk have just as many nutrients as whole milk. (When the fat is removed vitamin A is lost, but skim and low-fat milk must, by law, be fortified with the vitamin.) Most milk is fortified with vitamin D. If you are still growing, or are pregnant or lactating, it's wise to drink vitamin D fortified milk. Butter, cheese, and eggs are the only vegetarian foods that naturally contain more than a trace of the vitamin. Eggs are a fairly rich source of vitamin D.

The vitamin B12 content of dairy products can be important. You need at least 2 micrograms a day, and as you can see by looking at Appendix 6 most cheeses are not good sources. Milk, yogurt, and eggs are excellent sources.

Rennin is an enzyme used in cheese processing that makes possible the production of the insoluble curd characteristic of all hard or semihard cheeses. It is obtained only from slaughtered animals and thus is unacceptable to some vegetarians. Among domestic U.S. and Canadian cheeses, only ricotta is never made with rennin. Rennin is not used in the production of some small-curd cottage cheese. The only way to find out about the cottage cheese available in your area is to talk to the processor. Some imports, such as Alemtejo, a soft cheese from Portugal, are made without rennin.

## SOY MILK

If you depend on liquid or powdered fortified soy milk for vitamin B12 and calcium, check the label. Most brands don't supply adequate vitamin B12, so grind up half a tablet of the vitamin and add it to a quart of the beverage. The lowest potency tablet usually contains 25 micrograms, so in this way you will handily meet your requirement by drinking only one cup of soy milk a day. Fortified soy milk generally contains far less calcium than cow's milk. If you are concerned about calcium, add a scant teaspoon of calcium carbonate to each quart of beverage. This will provide approximately the same amount of calcium as cow's milk.

# NUTRITIONAL YEAST

Nutritional yeasts, such as brewer's yeast and torula yeast, are exceptionally high in nutrients. Many of them, however, have very large amounts of phorphorus and are comparatively low in calcium. A low ratio of calcium to phosphorus in the diet may, as we've seen in Chapter 6, promote osteoporosis. Several brands have a good calcium-phosphorus ratio (1:1 or better): Plus Formula 250, Plus Formula 450, Radiance Torula Yeast Powder (No. 691), and Radiance Super Brewer's Yeast (No. 692). If you get large amounts of calcium from other foods, the potential risk of eating a low-calcium/high-phosphorus yeast in moderate quantities is minimal.

# TEXTURED VEGETABLE PROTEIN

Textured vegetable protein (TVP) is a useful ingredient in vegetarian recipes. TVP is made from soybeans, which are fairly high in iron. In processing, the iron in most brands is largely lost. TVP, unlike soybeans, is low in fiber and contains little or no fat.

# HYDROGENATED FATS AND OILS

There has been some concern in recent years that the process of hydrogenation or hardening of fats and oils may have adverse health consequences. Hydrogenation produces an unnatural form of fatty acid called a *trans*-isomer, a form which some researchers consider highly suspect. In some, but not all, animal experiments, hydrogenated fat has been shown to contribute to atherosclerosis. An epidemiological study done in Great Britain shows a positive correlation between the amount of hydrogenated fat consumed and deaths from arteriosclerotic disease.

One of the chief sources of hydrogenated fat is margarine. Those who wish to cut down on their consumption of hydrogenated fat can make their own margarine. (See Recipes 37, 37A, and 37B in Chapter 14 for instructions.)

Many other processed foods, particularly those made with vegetable shortening (cakes and mixes, for example), contain substantial amounts of hydrogenated fat.

## WHICH FOODS ARE VEGETARIAN?

If you are serious about avoiding meat foods, you'll have to look at labels closely. Many canned soups are made with beef stock; gelatin, including Jell-O, comes from horses' hooves; Worcestershire sauce contains anchovies. Agar is a good (but expensive) substitute for gelatin, while some steak sauces (for example, A1 sauce) are completely plant based. Strict vegans have to be even more selective for even such staples as bread may contain nonfat dry milk. Some brands of bread such as Pepperidge Farm are made without milk.

## MULTIVITAMIN/MINERAL SUPPLEMENTS

If you follow a well-rounded lacto-vegetarian diet such as recommended in this book, there is no need to take a multivitamin/mineral supplement. Infants and some women have a need for iron supplements but these should be prescribed by a physician. Lacto-vegetarians ordinarily get sufficient vitamin D from milk and eggs. Additional amounts from a supplement could, in the opinion of some researchers, be harmful.

Vegans who drink commercially fortified soy milk are in effect already getting a multivitamin/mineral supplement and so there would be little point in taking a multivitamin/mineral capsule. The capsules are not a completely satisfactory substitute for fortified soy milk because they ordinarily don't contain much calcium.

## SALT IN FOODS

In Chapter 1 we discussed the desirability of limiting salt consumption. Virtually all processed foods have added salt, so if you are serious about keeping your sodium consumption low you would have to eat only unprocessed foods and those few processed items, such as frozen vegetables and a few of the breakfast cereals, that have no salt added. If this seems impractical, your next best option might be to avoid those foods which are particularly high in sodium, such as canned soups and such obviously oversalted items as pretzels, saltines, green olives, and prepared gravy mixes. Appendix 6 lists foods which are particularly high in sodium.

## SOME FOOD MYTHS

Misinformation about food is endemic. Most of it is harmless enough, but it is sometimes used to bamboozle the unsuspecting. Here are some of the more widespread myths:

*Cold-pressed oil is the best.* Cold-pressed oil is virtually unobtainable in America. Most oil labeled "cold pressed" is actually expeller pressed, a process that generates heat up to 160°F. Expeller pressing has no adverse effect on the quality of the oil. There is little evidence that refined oils sold in supermarkets are harmful.

*Sea salt is better than iodized salt because it supplies trace minerals.* There is no evidence that well-rounded diets based largely on unrefined foods lack trace elements. It is not clear how much of the trace elements there are in sea salt. (Notice that there is no declaration of content on the label.) Iodized salt provides adequate iodine for those who may not get enough of this nutrient from their food. The additives used in iodized salt are unlikely to have adverse effects.

*Organic food is superior to nonorganic.* There is no compelling evidence that organic produce (produce grown without benefit of pesticides and artificial fertilizers) is nutritionally superior to the nonorganic. In terms of pesticide contamination, organic produce may provide a real advantage. There is a French study published in 1974 showing that women on a diet of 70 percent or more organic foods had less than half the normal amount of pesticides in their breast milk. There's no standard for organic produce, so you can never be sure what you're getting if you buy it at a store. If you are thinking of growing your own, don't do it near well-traveled highways because toxic levels of lead from auto emissions may settle on the plants.

*Fertilized eggs are better than nonfertilized eggs.* Fertilized eggs contain slightly more hormones than the nonfertile, but otherwise they are chemically equal. Chicken hormones have no known function in human nutrition.

99

*Brown sugar, raw sugar, and honey are superior nutritionally to refined white sugar.* Brown sugar has marginally more nutrients than white sugar, but chemically it's just as pernicious. Raw sugar cannot legally be sold in stores. There is a branded product called *Sugar in the Raw* which is virtually the same as white sugar. Nutritionally, honey is little better than white sugar.

*Crude bran is a good source of fiber.* Crude bran is rich in hemicellulose but does not supply many of the other and possibly important components of fiber, such as pectin and lignin. Bran is high in phytic acid, a substance that binds with minerals, making them unavailable to the body. Bran also has a very large amount of phosphorus and very little calcium. A high phosphorus-calcium ratio in the diet over an extended period may contribute to the bone disease osteoporosis. Vegetarians and particularly vegans consume large amounts of fiber, so there is little point in adding it to vegetarian diets.

*Wheat germ, preferably raw, is the perfect food.* Wheat germ is an extremely nutritious food, but like crude bran it has a high phosphorus-calcium ratio and so may contribute to osteoporosis if used excessively. Raw wheat germ—usually found in health food stores—turns rancid more quickly than toasted wheat germ—usually found in supermarkets. The toasted wheat germ has more protein and is less expensive.

*Carob is superior to chocolate.* Carob contains substances called tannins, which have been found to depress the growth rate of animals. It is wise to limit children's consumption of carob candy and beverages.

*Yogurt promotes longevity.* This long-lived notion received a boost in recent years when researchers at the University of Nebraska reported that commercial yogurt inhibited cancerous tumors in mice. Despite this work, the protective effect of yogurt for humans remains unverified.

*Raw milk is superior to pasteurized milk.* Pasteurization destroys harmful organisms, such as those that cause tuberculosis, diphtheria, and other diseases. Advocates of raw milk claim that pasteurization destroys vitamins and naturally occurring enzymes. The modern method of pasteurization, called high-temperature–short-time pasteurization, destroys virtually none of the vitamins. There is no evidence that enzymes in milk are of any value to humans.

*Kelp is an excellent source of trace minerals.* The trace mineral content of kelp varies, but this seaweed is likely to be very high in iodine content. Excessive iodine taken over an extended period may cause goiter, so it is wise to limit consumption of kelp. A pinch or so a day is probably harmless.

*To live longer in better health, eliminate mucus-forming foods.* Some people who eat a lot of fruit believe that their diet is superior to all others because it eliminates mucus from the system. This theory was originally proposed by Arnold Ehret, an early twentieth-century food faddist. According to Ehret, all disease is caused by constipation. He claimed that by eating only those foods that don't form mucus—fruits, nuts, and green leafy vegetables—you'll loosen up the accumulated poisons of a lifetime from your colon. These poisons, according to his theory, are held there by mucus. Ehret's idea has no validity whatsoever. The mucus in the colon, far from holding poisons in the body, protects the colonic wall from abrasion and from the bacterial activity of the feces. Mucus holds the feces together and plays a vital role in their elimination, particularly during periods of intestinal stress. As Margaret, the nutritionist at The Farm, has so aptly put it, mucus "keeps you from squeaking, lets your food slip along the digestive tract, and keeps your nose moist."

*To promote good health, combine your foods properly at the same meal.* Many vegetarians believe that certain foods should not be combined in the same meal: green vegetables shouldn't be eaten with fruits; sweet fruits, such as bananas, should not be eaten with citrus fruits; melons should not be eaten with any other food. Apparently these notions are based on the assumption that primitive humans and prehumans did not eat these food combinations because they were not available naturally. The human digestive system, according to the theory, has not evolved to handle such "unnatural" combinations. There is no scientific evidence to either support or refute the theory.

*To avoid vitamin losses, don't cut your foods but eat them whole.* Some vegetarians believe that foods should not be cut up. It has been documented that slicing, mincing, grating, and shredding of vegetables and fruits does result in some losses of vitamin C and the B vitamins, due to exposure of inner surfaces to the air. The losses are minimal, particularly if you eat the food shortly after cutting.

# FASTING

Fasting may seem like a far-out practice, but I have not grouped it under food myths for it may have some value. There are experiments going back to early in the century showing that tumors don't grow in fasted laboratory mice. Clive McCay of Cornell University did many experiments in which a low-calorie diet greatly prolonged the life of animals, in some cases up to twice the normal span. Other researchers have found that total fasting for one day out of three increased the lifespan of rats by 15 to 20 percent and resulted in fewer tumors. Humans have experienced regression or slowing of local tumors on diets deficient in the amino acids phenylalanine and tyrosine. Hodgkin's disease and cancer of the uterus have also regressed with specific dietary restrictions. Some researchers have speculated that calorie restriction limits the nutrients needed for the growth of malignant cells.

It is not clear whether limited fasting has a beneficial effect for lean, normally healthy people. Obese people may benefit by fasting under a physician's guidance. Those who are moderately overweight but otherwise healthy may find occasional day-long fasts helpful in reducing.

If you are in good health, a day-long fast is unlikely to harm. Some healthy people have fasted for two weeks without permanent ill effect; but if you are trying it for more than a day or two, check with your doctor. Prolonged fasting may lead to health problems. For example, it results in uric acid accumulation in the blood and so may cause gout in susceptible individuals. In an experiment conducted for the United States Army, six healthy males, aged twenty-one to fifty-two, were put on a ten-day fast. Although they exercised strenuously, their physical performance was not impaired. However, their electrocardiograms became abnormal and one had such an abnormal electroencephalogram that the attending neurologist put him back on a normal diet for fear of possible seizure.

Some people believe that fasting is beneficial because it "cleans out the system" and so removes "accumulated poisons." It is true that you empty your alimentary tract during fasting, but whether this has any beneficial effect is not known.

Calorie restriction has a beneficial effect for many people, particularly the obese. Which method is better for limiting calories: short-term (one or two days) fasting or a consistent moderation? There is no evidence one way or another, but either way shouldn't be harmful if you are in good health.

# 11

## Simple Vegetarian Entrees

If you wish to follow a prudent vegetarian diet—one that is reasonably low in fat, cholesterol, and salt—you will probably find it convenient to emphasize dinner entrees like those in this chapter. Almost all of these recipes are based on beans. This is no accident. Most beans are low in fat and high in protein. The only important exception is soybeans, which, although exceptionally high in protein, are fairly high in fat. If you want to keep your fat consumption low, don't use soybeans exclusively.

The recipes in this chapter were chosen because they are easy to prepare. They will keep well in the refrigerator for at least two to three days and for considerably longer in the freezer. If recipes like these are staples of your diet, you may find it convenient to prepare double quantities and freeze half for later in the week.

There is nothing fancy about these recipes, yet they can be

very satisfying. Most beans are bland—some would say tasteless—yet this is their strength, because they can be flavored in an infinite variety of ways. Besides having the advantage of low cost, beans store well and are usually grown without pesticides.

Some people don't like beans, but don't forget that we are using the term broadly here to include garden peas and lima beans. Both of these can be used as the base for many of the recipes.

Beans are not essential to good lacto-vegetarian diet, but if you avoid them substitute other basic foods, particularly dairy products, cereals, and vegetables. On a vegan diet it is wise to emphasize the high-protein combination of beans and cereals particularly during the growth years and during pregnancy. In the recipes that follow, if instructions for cooking the beans are not shown on the package, refer to Table 8 in Chapter 10.

## ⇘ RECIPE 1 ⇙
### Basic Bean and Grain Casserole
*(6 servings)*

Choose one item from each of the four following groups:

1  cup raw beans, any type
½  cup raw rice or bulgar or 3 cups cooked corn
2  cups (= 10-ounce frozen packet) of any cooked vegetable—e.g., broccoli, spinach, carrots, mushrooms, eggplant, zucchini, asparagus, or string beans.
1  can condensed soup*—e.g., cream of mushroom, minestrone, vegetarian vegetable, etc., or vegetable stock

Cook beans, grain, and vegetable, and combine in large casserole dish. Add condensed soup or stock. This type of casserole is quite bland, so you'll want to flavor it heavily. Try 1 teaspoon onion powder, 1 teaspoon dry mustard, ½

---

* Most canned soups are extremely high in sodium. An alternate is low-sodium canned soup, usually available only in diluted form. Compensate for dilution by boiling off part of the water.

teaspoon thyme, ½ teaspoon dill, and ½ teaspoon garlic powder. Add:

1  large tomato, sliced thin and placed on top of casserole mixture
¼  cup cheese, grated—Parmesan, Romano, cheddar, or soy cheese—sprinkled on top

Bake casserole for 15–20 minutes in 350°F. oven.

*Nutrients per serving:* calories—270; protein—13 grams; fat—6 grams. (If made with soybeans: calories—295; protein—18 grams; fat—12 grams.)

RECIPE 2
## Bean Burgers
*(6 servings)*

You can make these in quantity and freeze for future use. Soybeans or any kind of beans plus oatmeal can be used as the base for bean burgers.

1  cup raw beans
1  cup uncooked oatmeal
½  cup nutritional yeast
½  teaspoon garlic powder
1  teaspoon dry mustard
1  teaspoon chili powder
1  teaspoon onion powder
2  tablespoons vegetable oil

Cook beans, mash, and combine with oatmeal, yeast, garlic, mustard, chili, and onion powder. Heat in oven for a few minutes at 300°F. (this inhibits soaking up oil during sautéing). Form into six thin burgers and fry in oil over low heat. Top with sliced onion and catsup and serve on bread or bun.

*Nutrients per burger:* calories—260; protein—17 grams; fat—6 grams. (If made with soybeans: calories—290; protein—21 grams; fat—11 grams.)

## ❧ RECIPE 3 ❦
## Bean-Nut Roast
### (10 servings)

2  cups raw beans
½ cup mixed nuts, chopped
2  cups onions, chopped
½ cup wheat germ
12-ounce can tomato paste
2  eggs (Vegans: substitute 2 tablespoons cornstarch plus 1
   tablespoon oil)
¼ teaspoon thyme
½ teaspoon oregano
¼ teaspoon basil
¼ teaspoon pepper
2  pats margarine

Cook beans and mash. Combine with other ingredients in
greased bread pan. Spread margarine on top and bake for 1½
hours at 300°F. Baste occasionally, adding water if too dry.
Let stand for 10–15 minutes before serving.

*Nutrients per serving:* calories—320; protein—16 grams;
fat—8 grams. (If made with soybeans: calories—350;
protein—16 grams; fat—14 grams.)

## ❧ RECIPE 4 ❦
## Old-Fashioned Baked Beans
### (6 servings)

2  cups raw navy beans
½ cup bean water
1  cup onions, chopped
4  tablespoons dark molasses
1  cup tomato sauce
1  tablespoon dry mustard
1  tablespoon steak sauce
1  tablespoon vinegar
8–12 tablespoons imitation bacon bits

Cook beans, reserving cooking water. Mix with other ingredients in well-greased casserole dish and bake covered for 9–10 hours at 300°F. If beans become too dry, add additional bean water. Serve with brown bread. Navy beans are the traditional ingredient in baked beans but other beans are palatable substitutes. Try limas, black beans, pintos, or soybeans.

*Nutrients per serving:* calories—285; protein—16 grams; fat—1 gram. (If made with soybeans: calories—310; protein—20 grams; fat—7 grams.)

## ⤶ RECIPE 5 ⤷
## Basic Bean Soup
### (6 servings)

This is a thick, hearty soup that is practically a meal in itself, and when eaten with bread or rolls, it gives you the benefit of complementary proteins.

2   cups raw beans, any type
4   cups onions, chopped
4   stalks celery, chopped
4   large carrots, chopped
4   tablespoons parsley
2   cloves garlic, minced
1   bay leaf
other seasonings to taste

Cook beans until semi-soft. Add other ingredients and cook until onions, celery, and carrots are soft. Puree about half the soup in a blender and add to remainder. Bean soup is quite bland, so you'll want to experiment by adding additional flavoring. Try a tablespoon of red wine or cider vinegar per cup. A small amount of sugar—one teaspoon or less—also adds flavor.

*Nutrients per serving:* calories—300; protein—18 grams; fat—1 gram. (If made with soybeans: calories—325; protein—22 grams; fat—7 grams.)

## ❧ RECIPE 6 ❦
## Fried Beans and Rice
### *(6 servings)*

1 cup raw garbanzo beans
3 cups onions, chopped
2 cloves garlic, minced
2 tablespoons vegetable oil
1½ cups wine
2 teaspoons ginger
2 cups raw rice, cooked according to directions

Cook beans. Heat chopped onions in oven for a few minutes at 300°F. Sauté onions and garlic in oil and small amount of wine until slightly brown. Add beans while still hot. Add ginger and remainder of wine, and simmer until beans are slightly brown. Pour over rice and serve. Kidney beans, pintos, and black beans are also tasty when fried.

*Nutrients per serving:* calories—400; protein—11 grams; fat—7 grams. (If made with soybeans: calories—425; protein—16 grams; fat—12 grams.)

## ❧ RECIPE 7 ❦
## Beans and Pasta
### *(6 servings)*

In this recipe, beans are used as the basis for vegetarian spaghetti sauce. Any type of bean can be used. My favorite, used in this recipe, is lentils.

1 cup raw lentils
1 cup onions, chopped
2 cloves garlic, minced
1 cup mushrooms, chopped
2 tablespoons vegetable oil
16-ounce can tomato sauce
2 teaspoons oregano
½ pound raw spaghetti, cooked

Cook lentils and puree in blender, adding tomato sauce as necessary to get liquid consistency. If necessary, add a few tablespoons of water. Preheat onions, garlic, and mushrooms in 300°F. oven for a few minutes and then sauté in oil until slightly brown. Add pureed beans, balance of tomato sauce, and oregano. Add to spaghetti.

*Nutrients per serving:* calories—360; protein—16 grams; fat—6 grams. (If made with soybeans: calories—385; protein—21 grams; fat—12 grams.)

## ⋙ RECIPE 8 ⋘
### Vegetable Casserole
*(6 servings)*

This recipe calls for one large or two small casserole dishes.

2   medium onions, boiled
3   large or 4 medium potatoes
10-ounce packet frozen cauliflower
10-ounce packet frozen string beans
10-ounce packet frozen peas
1   can condensed soup—cream type such as mushroom, celery, or asparagus. Vegans can substitute vegetarian vegetable or minestrone plus ½ cup concentrated soy milk.
½ cup nutritional yeast
1   large tomato, sliced thin

Preheat onions in 300°F. oven for a few minutes and then sauté in oil until slightly brown. Boil vegetables and potatoes until they are almost—but not quite—soft. Reserve vegetable cooking water. Combine onions, potatoes, vegetables, and soup in large bowl, adding about 1 cup of vegetable stock. Cover with sliced tomato, top with yeast, and bake in 350°F. oven for 10 minutes or until yeast begins to brown.

*Nutrients per serving:* calories—250; protein—16 grams; fat—5 grams.

# 12

## Favorite Gourmet Recipes

The dishes in this chapter are the kind that everyone seems to like, but with fancy foods such as these you pay a price in greater calorie and fat consumption. It's wise not to eat these dishes every day unless you're willing to give up other fatty foods — say, 4 or 5 pats of butter or the equivalent in other fats and oils. (See Table 2, Chapter 2.)

### ✒RECIPE 9✒
### Mushroom Omelette
*(3 servings)*

2   cups mushrooms, sliced
4   tablespoons onions, chopped
3   tablespoons butter or margarine
6   eggs, room temperature
⅛ teaspoon pepper

Preheat mushrooms and onions in 300°F. oven for a few minutes. Melt 2 tablespoons butter or margarine in large frying pan. Add mushrooms and onions and sauté until brown.

In separate large frying pan—preferably one with sloping sides—melt 1 tablespoon butter or margarine. Beat eggs, add 3 tablespoons water. Pour eggs into pan, stirring the surface with a fork. Allow edges to congeal—about 30 seconds—and then, tilting the pan slightly, coax the liquid egg on top to the edge of the pan and under the congealed part of the omelette. After no liquid is left on top, add mushrooms, slide omelette onto plate. Fold, divide in three parts, and serve.

*Nutrients per serving:* calories—290; protein—14 grams; fat—23 grams.

## RECIPE 10
### Spanish Omelette
*(3 servings)*

3   tablespoons butter or margarine
½ cup onions, minced
½ cup green peppers, minced
½ clove garlic, minced
1   16-ounce can stewed tomatoes
1   teaspoon sugar
⅛ teaspoon ground cloves
⅛ teaspoon pepper
1   bay leaf
6   eggs, room temperature

Melt 2 tablespoons butter or margarine in frying pan. Preheat onions, green peppers, and garlic in 300°F. oven for a few minutes and then simmer in pan for about 5 minutes. Add tomatoes, sugar, and spices, and simmer for about 40 minutes uncovered or until mixture thickens.

Prepare eggs as in Recipe 9 and add sauce.

*Nutrients per serving:* calories—320; protein—16 grams; fat—23 grams.

## ✥ RECIPE 11 ✥
## Cheddar Cheese Soufflé
### *(4 servings)*

4 tablespoons butter or margarine
2 cups milk
3 tablespoons flour
¼ pound cheddar cheese, chopped fine
pinch cayenne pepper
¼ teaspoon black pepper
4 eggs, room temperature, separated

In saucepan heat milk and 3 tablespoons butter or margarine. Slowly add flour and stir until sauce thickens. Add cheese and spices, stirring over low heat until cheese is melted. Remove from heat and pour sauce onto the slightly beaten egg yolks, stirring continuously. In separate bowl beat egg whites until they are stiff and then fold into the sauce. With remaining butter or margarine, grease a large casserole dish. Pour into dish and bake at 300°F. for 1¼ hours.

*Nutrients per serving:* calories—370; protein—19 grams; fat—25 grams.

## ✥ RECIPE 12 ✥
## Eggplant Parmigiana
### *(6 servings)*

1 eggplant, about 1 pound
¼ cup wheat germ or bread crumbs
2 eggs
4 tablespoons flour
4 tablespoons oil
1 can tomato sauce (15 ounces)
½ cup onions, minced
1 clove garlic, minced
2 teaspoons oregano
⅛ teaspoon basil
⅛ teaspoon pepper
½ pound mozzarella cheese, sliced thin
1 cup grated Parmesan cheese

Peel eggplant and cut into ½-inch-thick slices. Warm slices in 300°F. oven for a few minutes. Beat eggs with fork and mix in wheat germ. Dip slices of eggplant in flour and then in wheat germ-egg mixture and once again in flour. Sauté in oil over medium-low heat until brown and crisp on both sides. Combine tomato sauce and flavorings in saucepan. Bring to boil and then simmer for 20 minutes. Place slices of eggplant in roasting pan, cover with mozzarella cheese, followed by tomato sauce, and top with Parmesan cheese. Bake at 400°F. for 15 minutes.

*Nutrients per serving:* calories—250; protein—14 grams; fat—18 grams.

## ⤳RECIPE 13⤲
## Mushroom Quiche
### *(8 servings)*

1   pound mushrooms, chopped
1   cup onions, chopped
½ teaspoon ginger
4   teaspoons oil
3   teaspoons red wine
4   eggs, beaten
1   store-bought piecrust stick
½ pint heavy cream
4   ounces cheddar or Gruyère cheese, sliced thin

Warm mushrooms and onions in 300°F. oven for a few minutes. Add ginger and sauté in oil and wine for about 10 minutes in saucepan. Make piecrust according to directions on package, using a deep dish suitable for baking (capacity should be at least 1½ quarts). Gradually add eggs and cream to saucepan, stirring continuously. Pour into piecrust shell and top with cheese. Bake 35 minutes at 350°F.

*Nutrients per serving:* calories—380; protein—9 grams; fat—31 grams.

## ⇘RECIPE 14⇙
## Onion and Blue Cheese Quiche
### (8 servings)

1   cup onions, chopped
2   tablespoons oil
1   16-ounce can tomatoes, drained, or 3 fresh
1   teaspoon oregano
1   clove garlic, minced
⅛  teaspoon pepper
3   eggs, beaten
3   ounces blue cheese
1   store-bought piecrust stick
¼  cup Parmesan cheese, grated

Warm onions in 300°F. oven for a few minutes. Sauté in oil until slightly brown. Add tomatoes and spices. Gradually stir in eggs and blue cheese, using a wire whisk. Make piecrust according to directions on package using a deep dish suitable for baking (capacity should be at least 1½ quarts). Pour mixture into piecrust shell. Top with Parmesan cheese and bake at 350°F. for 35 minutes.

*Nutrients per serving:* calories—245; protein—8 grams; fat—17 grams.

## ⇘RECIPE 15⇙
## Vegetable Quiche
### (8 servings)

1   pound vegetable such as broccoli, asparagus, zucchini, or
    spinach
2   eggs, beaten
1½ cups milk
¼  teaspoon nutmeg
⅛  teaspoon pepper
1   store-bought piecrust stick
½  cup grated Parmesan cheese

Cook vegetable. Mix eggs thoroughly with milk and add seasonings. Make piecrust according to directions on package, using a deep dish suitable for baking (capacity should be at least 1½ quarts). Sprinkle half of Parmesan cheese onto piecrust, add cooked vegetable, egg-milk mixture, and top with remaining cheese. Bake 30 minutes at 350°F.

*Nutrients per serving:* calories—210; protein—10 grams; fat—12 grams.

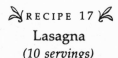

## RECIPE 16

## Bean Rarebit
### *(4 servings)*

½ cup raw pea (navy) beans, dry, cooked. Reserve cooking
   water.
1  15-ounce can tomato sauce
2  tablespoons oil
½ cup cheddar cheese, grated
½ cup nutritional yeast
1  teaspoon chili powder
dash hot pepper sauce
steak sauce to taste

Combine beans with tomato sauce and oil in blender. Add bean water as necessary to puree. Blend in cheese, yeast, and spices. Pour into saucepan, bring to boil, and then simmer for about 10 minutes. Pour over toast. Top with steak sauce.

*Nutrients per serving* (about ¾ cup of sauce over 2 slices of toast): calories—415; protein—27 grams; fat—17 grams.

## RECIPE 17

## Lasagna
### *(10 servings)*

12 lasagna noodles (or enough to cover your baking pan
   twice)
1  pound spinach or broccoli
1  15-ounce container ricotta cheese
2  eggs, beaten
½ pound mozzarella cheese, sliced thin
1  32-ounce jar spaghetti sauce
2  tablespoons parsley

Cook lasagna noodles al dente. Cook spinach (or broccoli), chop finely, and combine with ricotta and eggs. Place half of lasagna noodles in medium roasting pan, cover with half of vegetable-cheese-egg mixture, and then with half of mozzarella, and finally with half of spaghetti sauce. Repeat layers, top with parsley, and bake in preheated oven at 350°F. for 35 minutes.

*Nutrients per serving:* calories—310; protein—19 grams; fat—10 grams.

## RECIPE 18
### Ratatouille
*(8 servings)*

1   eggplant, about 1 pound, cut into 1-inch chunks, unpeeled
1   large zucchini, sliced ¼-inch thick
4   cups onions, chopped coarsely
4   medium tomatoes, cut into eighths
2   green peppers, chopped
1   small hot red pepper, finely chopped
1   pared cucumber, sliced ¼-inch thick
3   cloves garlic, minced
½ cup cooking oil
1   6-ounce can tomato paste
1   cup vegetable stock
½ cup dry red wine
½ cup parsley, chopped
¼ teaspoon basil
¼ teaspoon thyme

Warm eggplant, zucchini, onion, tomatoes, green peppers, red pepper, cucumber, and garlic in 300°F. oven for a few minutes. Heat oil in a large pot. Add warmed vegetables and stir until they are thoroughly coated. Simmer for 15 minutes, stirring occasionally. Add remaining items. Simmer for 45 minutes or until the vegetables are soft but not mushy. Stir occasionally. Serve as is or over rice.

*Nutrients per serving:* calories—225; protein—5 grams; fat—14 grams.

# 13

## Recipes
## for Sauces, Dips, and Beverages

Vegetables are virtuous but they have a reputation for dullness. You can make them more interesting by adding sauces like those in this chapter. Many of the sauces are also suitable for dressing up pasta and rice. For those who are watching their calories or fat consumption, the first two recipes—No. 19 and No. 20—are particularly useful. A double boiler should be used where indicated. One can be improvised by setting a stainless steel bowl over a saucepan. When using a double boiler, don't allow the boiling water to touch the upper pan. Another useful utensil in sauce making is a wire whisk for blending ingredients such as cheese.

If you are inclined to something sweet but abhor junk foods, try the low-fat beverages (Recipes 28 to 30). The first two are high in protein and so are particularly suitable for pregnant women.

The dip recipes are low in saturated fat (except for No. 35). Some of the dips can also be used as sandwich spreads although for this purpose you might want to allow somewhat less liquid in the preparation.

## ⤳RECIPE 19⤳
### Bean Sauce
*(about 3 cups, or 12 servings of 4 tablespoons each)*

1  cup raw pea (navy) beans
2  cups onions, chopped
2  cloves garlic, minced (optional)
4  tablespoons margarine or butter
1  cup skim milk or soy milk
¼  teaspoon pepper

Cook beans. Sauté onions and garlic (optional) in fat until soft but not browned. Combine beans and milk in blender. Blend in onions until smooth. Add pepper and warm in sauce. Use as is or for variety add one of the following:

2  tablespoons horseradish plus 1 tablespoon wine vinegar
½  tablespoon curry plus 1 tablespoon wine vinegar
6  tablespoons prepared mustard plus 1 tablespoon wine vinegar
2  cups tomato sauce* plus 2 tablespoons wine vinegar
1  cup red wine*

*Nutrients per serving:* calories—110; protein—5 grams; fat—4 grams.

## ⤳RECIPE 20⤳
### Cottage Cheese Sauce
*(about 2 cups, or 8 servings of 4 tablespoons each)*

1  cup cottage cheese, packed
1  cup skim milk
⅛  teaspoon pepper
.2  tablespoons cornstarch

* Using tomato sauce or red wine, yield is about 4 cups.

118

Combine first three ingredients in blender until smooth, then in saucepan bring almost to boil over high heat. Reduce heat. In small bowl add a few teaspoons of cold water to cornstarch—enough to make a thin paste. Slowly pour paste into saucepan, stirring vigorously with whisk. Stir frequently until mixture thickens—about 10 minutes. This mixture isn't too tasty by itself, so you'll want to add one of the flavorings below after mixture has thickened. Here are suggested amounts, which you may want to vary to suit individual taste.

1   tablespoon horseradish
½ teaspoon curry
¾ teaspoon powdered mustard
4–5 tablespoons tomato sauce
1   cup red wine*

*Nutrients per serving:* calories—50; protein—5 grams; fat—1 gram.

## ⤳RECIPE 21⤶
### Béchamel Sauce (White Sauce)
*(2 cups, or 8 servings of 4 tablespoons each)*

3   cups milk or soy milk
2   tablespoons grated onion
$1/16$ teaspoon nutmeg
4   peppercorns
3   tablespoons margarine or butter
4   tablespoons flour

Combine first four ingredients in saucepan and bring to boil. Remove from heat and let stand. Melt margarine or butter in pan, remove from heat, and slowly stir in flour until completely blended. Reheat butter-flour mixture until it begins to boil and then remove from heat again. Strain milk and blend in slowly with butter-flour mixture, using wire whisk. Bring to boil, reduce heat, and cook uncovered until volume is reduced to 2 cups—about 15–20 minutes. Béchamel is the starting point for a variety of satisfying

* Using red wine, yield is about 3 cups.

sauces, including the three recipes following, or it can be used as is on vegetables and potatoes.

*Nutrients per serving:* calories—115; protein—4 grams; fat—8 grams.

## ⨭RECIPE 22⨬
### Sour Cream Sauce
*(2 cups, or 8 servings of 4 tablespoons each)*

2  cups béchamel sauce (Recipe No. 21)
⅔ cups sour cream or soy sour cream (Recipe No. 41)
1  teaspoon lemon juice

Simmer béchamel sauce for about 5–10 minutes with frequent stirring. Add sour cream and lemon juice and bring to boil over medium heat. Remove from heat. Excellent on vegetables, including potatoes.

*Nutrients per serving:* calories—155; protein—4 grams; fat—11 grams.

## ⨭RECIPE 23⨬
### Egg Sauce
*(1½ cups, or 6 servings of 4 tablespoons each)*

1  cup béchamel sauce (Recipe No. 21)
¼ cup heavy cream
2  egg yolks
⅛ teaspoon pepper
2  tablespoons lemon juice
2  teaspoons parsley flakes

Put béchamel in saucepan for 5–10 minutes over medium heat, stirring frequently. In bowl blend cream and egg yolks and pepper with fork. Add béchamel to bowl, stirring constantly with wire whisk. Pour mixture into double boiler and heat but do not boil. Add lemon juice, parsley, and serve.

*Nutrients per serving:* calories—125; protein—4 grams; fat—10 grams.

## ⤳RECIPE 24⤶
### Mornay Sauce
*(1 ¼ cups, or 5 servings of 4 tablespoons each)*

1  cup béchamel sauce (Recipe No. 21)
3  tablespoons heavy cream
1  egg yolk
1  tablespoon grated Parmesan cheese
1  tablespoon grated Gruyère cheese
$1/16$ teaspoon cayenne

Put béchamel in double boiler over low heat for 5–10 minutes, stirring frequently. Blend cream and egg yolk in separate bowl. Gradually blend in half cup of béchamel sauce, stirring constantly with wire whisk. Return this mixture to rest of béchamel sauce. Over low heat, add cheese, stirring constantly with whisk until cheese is fully blended. Add cayenne and serve.

*Nutrients per serving:* calories—140; protein—5 grams; fat—10 grams.

## ⤳RECIPE 25⤶
### Cheddar Cheese Sauce
*(about 1 ¾ cups, or 7 servings of 4 tablespoons each)*

1  13-ounce can of evaporated milk
6  ounces mild cheddar cheese, cut fine
½  teaspoon dry mustard

Heat undiluted evaporated milk in double boiler. Add cheese and cover. Stir frequently until cheese melts—about 20 minutes. Stir in mustard.

*Nutrients per serving:* calories—175; protein—10 grams; fat—12 grams.

## ❧RECIPE 26❧

## Mock Hollandaise Sauce

*(about 1 cup, or 4 servings of 4 tablespoons each)*

1   cup buttermilk
1   teaspoon sugar
¼   teaspoon dry mustard
2   egg yolks
2   tablespoons margarine or butter
2   tablespoons lemon juice
⅛   teaspoon pepper

Heat first three ingredients in double boiler but do not boil.
In separate bowl beat egg yolks slightly and blend into part
of heated sauce. Return mixture to double boiler, add
remaining ingredients, and heat for 2–4 minutes, stirring
briskly. Do not boil.

*Nutrients per serving:* calories—105; protein—4 grams;
fat—8 grams.

## ❧RECIPE 27❧

## Blue Cheese Sauce

*(about 3 cups, or 12 servings of 4 tablespoons each)*

1   cup cottage cheese, creamed
½   cup milk
½   cup onions, minced
¼   teaspoon hot pepper sauce
1   teaspoon steak sauce
4   ounces blue cheese
1   cup sour cream

Combine first five ingredients in bowl. Add cheese, beating it in with a fork, and then fold in sour cream. Serve cold as a salad dressing or heat in covered double boiler for use on vegetables or potatoes.

*Nutrients per serving:* calories—105; protein—6 grams; fat—8 grams.


## ⁂RECIPE 28⁂
## High-Protein Drink for Lacto-Vegetarians
### *(3 cups)*

2 cups skim milk
1 ounce nonfat dry milk powder (about 5 tablespoons)
1 banana, ripe (or 1 cup any other fresh fruit)
2 tablespoons cocoa or carob powder
2 tablespoons nutritional yeast
½ teaspoon vanilla extract

Combine all ingredients in blender.

*Nutrients per cup:* calories—150; protein—12 grams; fat—1 gram.


## ⁂RECIPE 29⁂
## High-Protein Drink for Vegans
### *(3 cups)*

2 cups fortified soy milk (store-bought or Recipe 36)
1 ounce soy milk powder (about 5–6 tablespoons)
1 banana, ripe (or 1 cup any other fresh fruit)
2 tablespoons cocoa or carob powder
4 tablespoons nutritional yeast
½ teaspoon vanilla extract

Combine all ingredients in blender.

*Nutrients per cup:* calories—210; protein—11 grams; fat—7 grams.

## ❧ RECIPE 30 ❧
### Fruitshake
*(4 cups)*

2  bananas, ripe
3  cups orange juice

Combine in blender. Drink as is or freeze and use as ice cream substitute.

*Nutrients per cup:* calories—135; protein—2 grams; fat—0.5 grams.


## ❧ RECIPE 31 ❧
### Nut and Raisin Dip
*(about 2 ½ cups, or 5 servings of ½ cup each)*

⅓ cup raw garbanzo beans
¾ cup cashew nuts, minced
1  cup raisins
2  tablespoons nutritional yeast

Cook garbanzo beans, reserving cooking water. Blend into a mash using bean water as necessary. Blend in remaining ingredients. Refrigerate and serve cold.

*Nutrients per serving:* calories—260; protein—8 grams; fat—10 grams.


## ❧ RECIPE 32 ❧
### Garlic Dip
*(about 3 cups, or 6 servings of ½ cup each)*

1⅓ cups raw garbanzo beans
4  tablespoons salad oil
10 cloves garlic, minced
1  tablespoon chives
4  tablespoons parsley

Cook beans, reserving cooking water. Mix beans and oil in blender, adding bean water as necessary to blend. Mix in garlic and chives. Refrigerate. Serve cold topped with parsley.

*Nutrients per serving:* calories—145; protein—5 grams; fat—7 grams.

## ❧ RECIPE 33 ❦
## Date-Nut Dip
*(about 2 ½ cups, or 5 servings of ½ cup each)*

2  cups dates, chopped
½ cup black walnuts, chopped fine
2  teaspoons orange rind, grated
1  teaspoon ginger powder

Cover dates with boiling water and let stand until soft. In blender mix with other ingredients. Refrigerate and serve.

*Nutrients per serving:* calories—275; protein—4 grams; fat—8 grams.

## ❧ RECIPE 34 ❦
## Hummus
*(about 2 ½ cups, or 5 servings of ½ cup each)*

⅔ cup raw garbanzo beans
½ cup lemon juice
½ cup sesame butter (tahini)
2  cloves garlic, minced
3  tablespoons parsley flakes
½ teaspoon paprika

Cook beans, reserving cooking water. Place in blender with lemon juice and mix thoroughly, adding bean cooking water as necessary to blend. Blend in tahini and garlic. Place in bowl and refrigerate. Before serving, sprinkle with parsley.

*Nutrients per serving:* calories—185; protein—8 grams; fat—9 grams.

## ⋞RECIPE 35⋟
# Blue Cheese Dip
*(about 2 cups, or 4 servings of ½ cup each)*

½ cup raw garbanzo beans
4 ounces blue or Roquefort cheese
½ cup lemon juice
4 tablespoons chives, dried
4 tablespoons nutritional yeast

Cook beans. Blend all ingredients together, refrigerate, and serve.

*Nutrients per serving:* calories—220; protein—14 grams; fat—10 grams.

# 14

# Substitutes for Animal Foods:
# How to Prepare Them

This chapter is not only for vegans but for those who may want to cut down on saturated fats or simply want to try something new. If you like dairy products you may find the soy cheese and soy milk ice cream particularly satisfying.

### RECIPE 36
### Soy Milk
*(about 6 cups)*

To make soy milk at home and do it properly takes dedication. Unless you're willing to put in a fair amount of work for a fairly low return, I recommend store-bought soy milk.

The key to making tasty soy milk is to crush the beans in very hot water—180°F. or over. This method, which was developed by Dr. Malcolm Bourne of Cornell University, inactivates the enzyme lipoxidase, which is responsible for the bitter, beany flavor of soybeans.

- Soak 1 cup of soybeans in a pot for up to 16 hours in cold water. The soaked soybeans should fill approximately 2½ cups. Discard soaking water.
- Set aside half the beans from the pot and cover the remainder with boiling water.
- While beans are soaking in pot, fill a blender with very hot tap water and allow to stand for several minutes.
- Empty the blender and fill with boiling water. Allow to stand for several minutes and then discard water.
- Drain water from pot and put beans in blender. Add 2 cups of boiling water.
- Blend for 2–3 minutes. It will help to keep temperature over 180°F. if you insulate the blender with newspapers. If the top of your blender is plastic, protect it by covering the inside with aluminum foil.
- Place a colander over a deep pot. Place kitchen towel over colander. Filter blended soybeans through towel. Squeeze towel thoroughly to extract all of the liquid possible.
- Repeat process for remaining soybeans.
- You should now have about 4 cups of liquid. Place it in a double boiler and cook uncovered for 30–40 minutes, stirring frequently to avoid formation of skim.
- The remaining liquid—about 3 cups—can be used as soybean cream. To make soybean milk, add 3 cups of water. To make the beverage tasty, add, for each batch, 2 or 3 tablespoons of sugar, honey, corn syrup, or table syrup, ½ teaspoon of vanilla, and 2 tablespoons of oil. If you want a low-calorie beverage, eliminate the oil.
- To fortify, add to each batch of 6 cups: 1 tablespoon of calcium carbonate; a 25-microgram tablet of vitamin B12 (crushed); and a 25-milligram tablet of riboflavin. This will give you far more vitamin B12 and riboflavin per cup than needed to satisfy your daily requirements. These vitamins aren't ordinarily available in smaller units but the excess over requirement is not harmful. If children are drinking the soymilk in place of cow's milk, add a 400 I.U. tablet of vitamin D during the winter months or when they get little sunshine.

• Refrigerate immediately. Soy milk will keep up to five days in the refrigerator.

*Nutrients per cup:* calories—135; protein—8 grams; fat—8 grams. (Without added oil: calories—95; protein—8 grams; fat—3 grams.)

## RECIPE 37
## Soy Margarine
*(about 1 pound)*

1  cup soy flour
1  cup water
1½ cups peanut oil
2  tablespoons carrot juice
1½ teaspoons imitation butter flavor

Cook soy flour and water in double boiler until thick—about 20–30 minutes. Blend in remaining ingredients thoroughly, using a wire whisk. Refrigerate.

*Nutrients in 1 teaspoon* (= 1 pat): calories—35; protein—trace; fat—4 grams.

The following two recipes are for lacto-vegetarians and have about the same nutritional content as Recipe 37.

## RECIPE 37A
*(about 1 pound)*

Same as Recipe 37 except substitute equal amount of instant nonfat dry milk for soy flour.

## RECIPE 37B
*(about 1 pound)*

2  8-ounce sticks butter
1  cup corn or safflower oil

Soften butter at room temperature for an hour or so. Combine with oil in blender and refrigerate. This spread has a better P/S (polyunsaturated/saturated fatty acid) ratio than regular butter. (The P/S ratio of regular butter is .04 to 1.0; spread made with corn oil has a P/S ratio of 0.9 to 1.0; spread made with safflower oil has a P/S ratio of 1.4 to 1.0.)

Recipes 37, 37A, and 37B are useful for those who wish to avoid the possible hazard of *trans*-isomers, present in the hydrogenated fat of commercial margarine. (See Chapter 10.)

## RECIPE 38
### Soy Cheese
*(about 14 ounces)*

8   ounces margarine
1   cup powdered soy milk
4   tablespoons nutritional yeast
4   tablespoons lemon juice
¼   teaspoon garlic powder

Melt margarine in saucepan over low heat. Blend in remaining ingredients. Beat until smooth. Refrigerate until hard.

*Nutrients in 1 ounce:* calories—145; protein—3 grams; fat—12 grams.

## RECIPE 39
### Soy Mayonnaise
*(about 19 ounces)*

1   13-ounce can concentrated soy milk
1   tablespoon sugar
½   teaspoon onion powder
¼   teaspoon garlic powder
¼   teaspoon paprika
¾   cup peanut oil
3–4 tablespoons lemon juice

Place the soy milk, sugar, onion powder, garlic powder, and paprika in blender and whip until foamy. Blend in oil gradually. Add lemon juice. Refrigerate.

*Nutrients in 1 tablespoon:* calories—31; protein—1 gram; fat—3 grams.

## ⚘RECIPE 40⚘
## Soy Whipped Topping
### *(about 17 ounces)*

1 13-ounce can concentrated soy milk
1 teaspoon vanilla
1½ teaspoons sugar
½ cup oil
1½ to 3 tablespoons lemon juice

It's better to use chilled soy milk, oil, and lemon juice. Place soy milk, vanilla, and sugar in blender and whip. Blend in oil gradually. Add lemon juice until mixture thickens.

*Nutrients in 2 tablespoons whipped:* calories—90; protein—1 gram; fat—8 grams.

## ⚘RECIPE 41⚘
## Soy Sour Cream
### *(about 1 pound)*

1 13-ounce can concentrated soy milk
1 teaspoon sugar
4 tablespoons oil
1½ tablespoons lemon juice

Mix soy milk and sugar in blender. Blend in oil slowly. Add lemon juice and refrigerate.

*Nutrients in 2 tablespoons:* calories—50; protein—1 gram; fat—3 grams.

## ❧RECIPE 42❧
## Soy Milk Ice Cream
*(about 3 pints)*

1   13-ounce can concentrated soy milk
6   tablespoons water
6   tablespoons peanut oil
6   tablespoons sugar
2   small bananas
½   teaspoon vanilla

Place soymilk and water in blender and whip. Blend in oil slowly. Add sugar, bananas, and vanilla. Pour in ice cube trays and put in freezer for 15–20 minutes or until partially frozen. Whip again in blender. This helps prevent ice slivers from forming. Freeze again until hard.

Variations: Sliced peaches, strawberries, and other berries can be used in place of bananas. In place of sugar use 2 to 8 tablespoons of pancake syrup. Most commercially made soy milk is sweetened, so you may wish to compensate by using less sweetener.

*Nutrients per ½ cup:* calories—145; protein—3 grams; fat—7 grams.

# APPENDIXES

APPENDIX 1

# Nutrients in Typical Vegetarian Menus

The typical menus shown in Table A are based on the suggested minimum servings recommended in this book. These menus are designed to illustrate that vegetarian diets—both lacto-vegetarian and vegan—can satisfy normal nutritional requirements.

Table B shows the nutrient composition of the typical menus. The composition was calculated using the assumption that no supplements or fortified foods are included. This was done in order to illustrate where vegetarian diets are apt to be deficient. As you can see, the vegan diets, as measured against the American RDA, are deficient in calcium for all groups except adult males. (As measured against the lower levels set by the World Health Organization, only infants and pregnant and lactating women would be deficient.) Vegan diets, of course, supply no vitamin B12. *In practice, these deficiencies would be overcome by drinking fortified soy milk.* The table also illustrates that infants and pregnant women— both lacto-vegetarian and vegan—get insufficient iron from their diets and therefore need a supplemental supply. (This is true of omnivores also.)

## TABLE A
### Typical Vegetarian Menus

| *Lacto-Vegetarian* | *Vegan* |
|---|---|

### *Infants 6 to 12 months —970 calories*

| Lacto-Vegetarian | Vegan |
|---|---|
| 1/3 cup oatmeal | 1/3 cup oatmeal |
| 1 slice whole-wheat bread | 1 slice whole-wheat bread |
| 2 cups whole milk | 2 cups soy milk |
| 4 ounces orange juice | 4 ounces orange juice |
| 1/2 tablespoon peanut butter | 1/2 tablespoon peanut butter |
| 1/3 cup beans | 1/2 cup beans |
| 1/2 cup broccoli | 1/2 cup broccoli |
| 1/2 cup kale | 1/2 cup kale |
| 1/2 banana | 1/2 banana |
| 1/2 cup summer squash | 1/2 cup summer squash |
| 1/2 large potato | 1/2 large potato |

### *Children 4 to 6 years —1800 calories*

| Lacto-Vegetarian | Vegan |
|---|---|
| *Breakfast:* 1/2 cup oatmeal, 1 slice toast, 1 poached egg, 1 cup skim milk, 4 ounces orange juice | *Breakfast:* 1/2 cup oatmeal, 1 slice toast, 1 cup soy milk, 4 ounces orange juice |
| *Lunch:* 1 cup vegetable soup, 1 peanut butter and banana sandwich, 1 cup whole milk, 1 oatmeal cookie | *Lunch:* 1 cup vegetable soup, 1 peanut butter sandwich, 1 cup soy milk, 1 oatmeal cookie |
| *Dinner:* 1/2 cup beans, 1 large potato, 1 cup broccoli, small salad, 1 slice bread, 1 cup whole milk, banana | *Dinner:* 3/4 cup beans, 1 large potato, 1 cup broccoli, small salad, 1 slice bread, 1 cup soy milk, banana |
| *Snack:* Apple | *Snack:* Apple |

### *Males 11 to 14 years —2800 calories*

| Lacto-Vegetarian | Vegan |
|---|---|
| *Breakfast:* 1 cup oatmeal, 1 cup skim milk, toasted muffin with jam, 1 boiled egg, 6 ounces orange juice | *Breakfast:* 1 cup oatmeal, 1 cup soy milk, toasted muffin with jam, 6 ounces orange juice |
| *Lunch:* Peanut butter and jelly sandwich, 1 cup skim milk, 1 ounce pound cake | *Lunch:* Large salad with 1 cup garbanzo beans, 2 slices bread, 1 cup soy milk, 1 1/2 ounces fruitcake |
| *Dinner:* 1 cup beans, 2 slices bread, 1 cup broccoli, large salad, large potato, 1 cup sherbet | *Dinner:* 1 cup beans, 2 slices bread, 1 cup broccoli, 1 cup summer squash, 1 large potato |
| *Snacks:* Banana, 1 cup plain yogurt, 5 rye wafers with 1 ounce cheddar cheese | *Snacks:* Apple, banana, pear, 6 rye wafers, 1/2 cup soy ice cream, 1/2 ounce peanuts |

| Lacto-Vegetarian | Vegan |
|---|---|

### Males 23 to 50 years—2700 calories

*Breakfast:* 1 cup oatmeal, 1 cup skim milk, toasted muffin with jam, 6 ounces orange juice, coffee or tea

*Lunch:* Peanut butter and jelly sandwich, 1 cup skim milk, 1 ounce pound cake

*Dinner:* 1 cup beans, 2 slices bread, 1 cup broccoli, large salad, 1 large potato, 1 cup sherbet, coffee or tea

*Snacks:* Banana, 1 cup yogurt, 5 rye wafers with 1 ounce cheddar cheese

*Breakfast:* 1 cup oatmeal, 1 cup soy milk, toasted muffin with jam, 6 ounces orange juice, coffee or tea

*Lunch:* Large salad with 1 cup garbanzo beans, 2 slices bread, 1 cup soy milk, 1½ ounces fruitcake

*Dinner:* 1 cup beans, 2 slices bread, 1 cup broccoli, 1 cup summer squash, 1 large potato, coffee or tea

*Snacks:* Apple, banana, pear, 6 rye wafers, ½ cup soy ice cream

### Males over 50—2400 calories

*Breakfast:* 1 cup oatmeal, 1 cup skim milk, toasted muffin with jam, 6 ounces orange juice, coffee or tea

*Lunch:* Large salad with one cup uncreamed cottage cheese, 2 slices bread, banana

*Dinner:* 1 cup beans, 1 cup broccoli, 1 large potato, 2 slices bread, coffee or tea

*Snacks:* 1 cup plain yogurt, 1 cup skim milk, peanut butter sandwich

*Breakfast:* 1 cup oatmeal, 1 cup soy milk, toasted muffin with jam, 6 ounces orange juice, coffee or tea

*Lunch:* Large salad with 1 cup garbanzo beans, 2 slices bread, 1 cup soy milk

*Dinner:* 1 cup beans, 2 slices bread, 1 cup broccoli, 1 cup summer squash, 1 large potato, coffee or tea

*Snacks:* Apple, banana, pear, 6 rye wafers

### Female 11 to 14 years—2400 calories

*Breakfast:* 1 cup oatmeal, 1 cup skim milk, 1 egg, toasted muffin with jam, 6 ounces orange juice

*Lunch:* Peanut butter sandwich, 1 cup skim milk, 1 ounce pound cake

*Dinner:* 1 cup beans, 1 cup broccoli, large salad, 1 large potato, 2 slices bread, 1 ounce cheese

*Snacks:* Apple, banana, 1 cup plain yogurt, 1 doughnut

*Breakfast:* 1 cup oatmeal, 1 cup soy milk, toasted muffin with jam, 6 ounces orange juice

*Lunch:* Peanut butter sandwich, 1 cup soy milk, ½ cup soy ice cream

*Dinner:* 1 cup beans, 1 cup kale, large salad, 1 large potato, 2 slices bread, 1½ ounces fruitcake

*Snacks:* Apple, banana, 5 rye wafers

| Lacto-Vegetarian | Vegan |
|---|---|

### Females 23 to 50 years—2000 calories

**Breakfast:** 1 cup oatmeal, toasted muffin, 1 egg, 1 cup skim milk, 6 ounces orange juice, coffee or tea
**Lunch:** Peanut butter sandwich, 1 cup skim milk, banana
**Dinner:** 1 cup beans, 1 stalk broccoli, large salad, 2 slices bread, 1 cup plain yogurt, coffee or tea
**Snack:** Apple

**Breakfast:** 1 cup oatmeal, toasted muffin, 1 cup soy milk, 6 ounces orange juice, coffee or tea
**Lunch:** Peanut butter sandwich, 1 cup soy milk, banana
**Dinner:** 1 cup beans, 1 cup kale, large salad, 1 large potato, 2 slices bread, coffee or tea
**Snack:** Apple, 3 rye wafers

### Pregnancy—2300 calories

**Breakfast:** 1 cup oatmeal, 1 cup skim milk, toasted muffin, 6 ounces orange juice
**Lunch:** Large salad with 1 cup garbanzo beans and 1 boiled egg, 1 cup skim milk, banana
**Dinner:** 1 cup beans, 1 cup broccoli, large potato, 2 slices bread, 1 cup skim milk
**Snacks:** Peanut butter sandwich, 1 cup plain yogurt, apple

**Breakfast:** 1 cup oatmeal, 1 cup soy milk, toasted muffin, 6 ounces orange juice
**Lunch:** Large salad with 1 cup garbanzo beans, 2 slices bread, 1 cup soy milk
**Dinner:** 1 cup beans, 1 cup broccoli, 1 cup kale, 2 slices bread, large potato, 1 cup soy milk
**Snacks:** Apple, 1 cup soy milk, 4 rye wafers

### Lactation—2500 calories

Same as pregnancy plus 1 ounce pound cake and extra teaspoon salad oil

Same as pregnancy plus 1 banana, 2 additional rye wafers, extra pat of margarine

### Females over 50—1800 calories

**Breakfast:** 1 cup oatmeal, 1 cup skim milk, 1 egg, toasted muffin, 6 ounces orange juice, coffee or tea
**Lunch:** Large salad with 1 cup uncreamed cottage cheese, 1 cup skim milk
**Dinner:** 1 cup beans, 1 cup broccoli, 2 slices bread, 1 large potato, coffee or tea, banana
**Snacks:** Apple, 1 cup plain yogurt

**Breakfast:** 1 cup oatmeal, 1 cup soy milk, toasted muffin, 6 ounces orange juice, coffee or tea
**Lunch:** Peanut butter sandwich, 1 cup soy milk, banana
**Dinner:** 1 cup beans, 1 cup kale, large salad, 1 large potato, 2 slices bread, coffee or tea
**Snack:** Apple

Note: In the menus detailed above it is assumed that for each slice of bread and each portion of vegetable, one pat of corn oil margarine is used. For each large salad, in the lacto-vegetarian menus up to one tablespoon of corn oil is used and in the vegan menus up to one tablespoon of olive oil. The large salads include 1 cup of lettuce (55g), ½ tomato (50g), one stalk of celery (17g), and ½ carrot (40g). The small salads include half these amounts. All bean portions are on cooked basis.

## TABLE B
### Nutrient Composition of Typical Vegetarian Menus[1]

| | | Calories | Percent of Allowance[2] | | | | | | | | | Percent of Total Calories | | |
| | | | Protein | Calcium | Iron[3] | Vitamin A | Thiamin | Riboflavin | Niacin[4] | Vitamin B12 | Vitamin C | Total Fat | Saturated Fat | Poly-unsaturated Fat |
|---|---|---|---|---|---|---|---|---|---|---|---|---|---|---|
| | | | % | % | % | % | % | % | % | % | % | % | % | % |
| **Lacto-Vegetarian** | | | | | | | | | | | | | | |
| Infants | 6–12 mos. | 970 | 210 | 160 | 40[5] | 435 | 385 | 225 | 95 | 600 | 625 | 37 | 12 | 9 |
| Children | 4– 6 yrs. | 1800 | 255 | 165 | 150 | 475 | 160 | 210 | 135 | 245 | 700 | 32 | 9 | 8 |
| Males | 11–14 yrs. | 2800 | 230 | 140 | 115 | 245 | 135 | 185 | 95 | 150 | 695 | 30 | 8 | 9 |
| Males | 23–50 yrs. | 2700 | 170 | 210 | 200 | 235 | 135 | 165 | 95 | 115 | 695 | 29 | 8 | 9 |
| Males | Over 50 | 2400 | 200 | 195 | 200 | 225 | 155 | 190 | 110 | 145 | 685 | 27 | 7 | 9 |
| Females | 11–14 yrs. | 2400 | 210 | 135 | 105 | 305 | 155 | 205 | 95 | 145 | 700 | 31 | 10 | 8 |
| Females | 23–50 yrs. | 2000 | 180 | 175 | 100 | 295 | 180 | 205 | 110 | 135 | 700 | 28 | 6 | 9 |
| Females | Pregnancy | 2300 | 140 | 150 | 5 | 235 | 160 | 200 | 105 | 125 | 530 | 25 | 6 | 8 |
| Females | Lactation | 2500 | 160 | 155 | 125 | 200 | 160 | 180 | 95 | 125 | 400 | 28 | 7 | 9 |
| Females | Over 50 | 1800 | 215 | 180 | 165 | 285 | 170 | 255 | 90 | 175 | 700 | 21 | 5 | 7 |
| **Vegans** | | | | | | | | | | | | | | |
| Infants | 6–12 mos. | 970 | 180 | 75 | 70[5] | 410 | 205 | 115 | 105 | 6 | 610 | 38 | 6 | 14 |
| Children | 4– 6 yrs. | 1800 | 220 | 70 | 200 | 430 | 195 | 100 | 140 | 6 | 395 | 29 | 5 | 11 |
| Males | 11–14 yrs. | 2800 | 205 | 70 | 170 | 250 | 180 | 115 | 110 | 6 | 765 | 29 | 5 | 10 |
| Males | 23–50 yrs. | 2700 | 155 | 105 | 300 | 250 | 175 | 105 | 95 | 6 | 765 | 27 | 5 | 9 |
| Males | Over 50 | 2400 | 145 | 100 | 275 | 250 | 190 | 105 | 100 | 6 | 760 | 25 | 5 | 8 |
| Females | 11–14 yrs. | 2400 | 165 | 65 | 135 | 420 | 170 | 100 | 105 | 6 | 615 | 31 | 6 | 10 |
| Females | 23–50 yrs. | 2000 | 140 | 85 | 120 | 415 | 185 | 95 | 120 | 6 | 605 | 30 | 6 | 10 |
| Females | Pregnancy | 2300 | 120 | 85 | 5 | 405 | 195 | 105 | 105 | 6 | 665 | 29 | 5 | 10 |
| Females | Lactation | 2500 | 145 | 85 | 175 | 345 | 200 | 100 | 100 | 6 | 685 | 29 | 5 | 10 |
| Females | Over 50 | 1800 | 135 | 85 | 200 | 405 | 175 | 90 | 125 | 6 | 605 | 29 | 5 | 11 |

1. Based on menus on preceding pages.
2. All allowances are from Recommended Dietary Allowance, Eighth Edition (Washington: National Academy of Sciences, 1974).
3. Iron from plant foods is less well absorbed than iron from animal foods, hence recommended allowances may understate requirement for vegetarians.
4. Does not include niacin equivalents supplied by amino acid tryptophan. If equivalents are included, requirement is satisfied in all cases.
5. Amount does not satisfy Allowance. Standard practice is to supplement with iron.
6. Plant foods ordinarily supply little or no vitamin B12.

# Where to Buy Vegetarian Foods —

# A Short List of Processors and Wholesalers Who Sell by Mail

Co-op stores usually have a better selection of beans and grains than other stores. If you don't have one nearby, you might consider buying directly from a processor or wholesaler. Many of those listed below sell only in fairly large quantities—10- or 25-pound containers, for example. If you write for their listings you'll find that some list "organic" beans or grains at a higher price than the regular. There is little point in paying a premium for the organic type. Beans are usually raised with little or no pesticides and it's unclear whether grains normally contain significant amounts of pesticides.

*California*

El Molino Mills
P.O. Box 2025
Alhambra, Calif. 91803
(213) 686-2470

Westbrae Natural Foods, Inc.
1224   10th Street
Berkeley, Calif. 94710
(415) 658-7518

Kahan & Lessin Co.
3131 East Maria Street
Compton, Calif. 90221
(213) 631-5121

Erewhon Trading Co., Inc.
8454 Steller Drive
Culver City, Calif. 90230
(213) 836-7569

Nature's Best, Inc.
615 North Nash
El Segundo, Calif. 90245
(213) 772-7373

The Well
795 West Hedding Street
San Jose, Calif. 95126
(408) 247-4800

Harmony Foods
232 Amat Street
Santa Cruz, Calif. 95060
(408) 426-5021

Giusto's Specialty Foods
241 East Harris Avenue
South San Francisco, Calif. 94080
(415) 873-6566

*Colorado*

Colorado Specialty Foods Corp.
4430 Glencoe
Denver, Colo. 80216
(303) 371-3354

*Florida*

Mother Earth
604 N.W. 13th
Gainesville, Fla. 32601
(904) 378-5224

Akin Distributors, Inc.
1501 Commonwealth Ave.
Jacksonville, Fla. 32203
(904) 783-0420

Happy Health Products
7875 N.W. 77th Avenue
Miami, Fla. 33137
(305) 888-9701

Sun Ray Products, Inc.
169 N.W. 23rd Street
Miami, Fla. 33132
(305) 573-9141

Tree of Life, Inc.
315 Industrial Boulevard
St. Augustine, Fla. 32084
(904) 829-3484

*Illinois*

Fearn Soya Foods
4520 James Place
Melrose Park, Ill. 60160
(312) 345-2335

Vegetarian, Inc.
1310 West Main
Urbana, Ill. 61801
(217) 328-1656

*Massachusetts*

Erewhon Trading Co., Inc.
33 Farnsworth Street
Boston, Mass. 02210
(617) 542-1358

*Michigan*

Eden Foods
211 South State Street
Ann Arbor, Mich. 48108
(313) 973-9400

*Minnesota*
The Pavo Co.
119 North 4th Street
Minneapolis, Minn. 55401
(612) 339-6397

Gourmet Foods, Inc.
1020 Raymond Avenue
St. Paul, Minn. 55114
(612) 646-2981

*Nebraska*
Brownville Mills
Brownville, Nebr. 68321
(402) 825-4131

*New Jersey*
Balanced Foods, Inc.
2500  83rd St.
North Bergen, N.J. 07047
(201) 869-4400

Mottell Health Foods, Inc.
Linden, N.J. 07036
(201) 486-7477
N.Y.C.: (212) 925-9933

*New York*
Shadowfax Food Corp.
303 Crandall
Binghamton, N.Y.
(607) 723-5446

Agress Nut & Seed Co.
3632 Kingsbridge Avenue
Bronx, N.Y. 10563
(212) 548-2313

Regina Nut Products Corp.
180 Atlantic Avenue
Brooklyn, N.Y. 11201
(212) 439-5606

Graham Co.
39 Clarkson Street
New York, N.Y. 10014
(212) WA 4-0300

The Infinity Co., Inc.
173 Duane Street

New York, N.Y. 10013
(212) 966-3241

Mottell Health Foods, Inc.
Linden, N.J. 07036
(201) 486-7477
N.Y.C. (212) 925-9933

Sherman Foods, Inc.
276 Jackson Avenue
New York, N.Y. 10454
(212) 993-8900

*Oregon*
Nu Vita Foods
7524 S.W. Macadam Avenue
Portland, Oreg. 97214
(503) 246-5433

*Pennsylvania*
Walnut Acres
Penns Creek, Pa. 17862
(717) 837-6591

*Tennessee*
Collegedale Distributors
Olltewah, Tenn. 37315
(615) 238-4121

Life Line Foods
Rt. 4, Box 235
Pikesville, Tenn. 37367
(615) 881-3740

*Texas*
Good Food People, Inc.
2320 Rutland Drive
Austin, Tex. 78757
(512) 837-5613

Good Food Store
1101 West 5th
Austin, Tex. 78703
(512) 472-1942

*Wisconsin*
Essential Foods Co., Inc.
2023 West Wisconsin Avenue
Milwaukee, Wis. 53233
(414) 933-2100

# Recommended Dietary Allowances

The first table (Table C) shows the Recommended Dietary Allowances published by the National Academy of Sciences–National Research Council. It is a useful tool, but not everyone accepts it as the gospel.

Among those who have important disagreements with the RDA is the group of experts who've promulgated the World Health Organization recommendations (Table D). The two sets of recommendations differ importantly (at least for some age and sex groups) with respect to calcium, iron, vitamin B12, vitamin A, vitamin D, protein, and calories.

You could build a case for claiming that the WHO standards are somewhat more applicable to vegetarians, but as this edition is primarily for Americans I've used the National Research Council RDAs. The WHO recommendations serve as a useful reminder that nutrient recommendations shouldn't be engraved on stone.

For Canadian readers, the Recommended Daily Nutrient Intake as published by the Minister of Supply and Services is also included.

If you are interested in checking out the nutrient values of your diet against the standards, I recommend that you get a copy of *Nutritive Value of American Foods, Agriculture Handbook No. 456* (Washington: United States Department of Agriculture, 1975). It is available from the Superintendent of Documents, U.S. Government Printing Office, Washington, D.C. 20402.

## TABLE C

### Food and Nutrition Board, National Academy of Sciences—National Research Council
### Recommended Daily Dietary Allowances,[1] Revised 1974

*Designed for the maintenance of good nutrition of practically all healthy people in the U.S.A.*

| | Age (years) | Weight (kg) | Weight (lbs) | Height (cm) | Height (in) | Energy (kcal)[2] | Protein (g) | Vitamin A Activity (RE)[3] | (IU) | Vita-min D (IU) | Vita-min E Activity[5] (IU) | Ascor-bic Acid (mg) | Fola-cin[6] (µg) |
|---|---|---|---|---|---|---|---|---|---|---|---|---|---|
| Infants | 0.0-0.5 | 6 | 14 | 60 | 24 | kg ×117 | kg × 2.2 | 420* | 1,400 | 400 | 4 | 35 | 50 |
| | 0.5-1.0 | 9 | 20 | 71 | 28 | kg ×108 | kg × 2.0 | 400 | 2,000 | 400 | 5 | 35 | 50 |
| Children | 1-3 | 13 | 28 | 86 | 34 | 1,300 | 23 | 400 | 2,000 | 400 | 7 | 40 | 100 |
| | 4-6 | 20 | 44 | 110 | 44 | 1,800 | 30 | 500 | 2,500 | 400 | 9 | 40 | 200 |
| | 7-10 | 30 | 66 | 135 | 54 | 2,400 | 36 | 700 | 3,300 | 400 | 10 | 40 | 300 |
| Males | 11-14 | 44 | 97 | 158 | 63 | 2,800 | 44 | 1,000 | 5,000 | 400 | 12 | 45 | 400 |
| | 15-18 | 61 | 134 | 172 | 69 | 3,000 | 54 | 1,000 | 5,000 | 400 | 15 | 45 | 400 |
| | 19-22 | 67 | 147 | 172 | 69 | 3,000 | 54 | 1,000 | 5,000 | 400 | 15 | 45 | 400 |
| | 23-50 | 70 | 154 | 172 | 69 | 2,700 | 56 | 1,000 | 5,000 | | 15 | 45 | 400 |
| | 51+ | 70 | 154 | 172 | 69 | 2,400 | 56 | 1,000 | 5,000 | | 15 | 45 | 400 |
| Females | 11-14 | 44 | 97 | 155 | 62 | 2,400 | 44 | 800 | 4,000 | 400 | 12 | 45 | 400 |
| | 15-18 | 54 | 119 | 162 | 65 | 2,100 | 48 | 800 | 4,000 | 400 | 12 | 45 | 400 |
| | 19-22 | 58 | 128 | 162 | 65 | 2,100 | 46 | 800 | 4,000 | 400 | 12 | 45 | 400 |
| | 23-50 | 58 | 128 | 162 | 65 | 2,000 | 46 | 800 | 4,000 | | 12 | 45 | 400 |
| | 51+ | 58 | 128 | 162 | 65 | 1,800 | 46 | 800 | 4,000 | | 12 | 45 | 400 |
| Pregnant | | | | | | +300 | +30 | 1,000 | 5,000 | 400 | 15 | 60 | 800 |
| Lactating | | | | | | +500 | +20 | 1,200 | 6,000 | 400 | 15 | 80 | 600 |

| | Age (years) | Nia-cin[7] (mg) | Ribo-flavin (mg) | Thia-min (mg) | Vita-min B6 (mg) | Vita-min B12 (μg) | Cal-cium (mg) | Phos-phorus (mg) | Iodine (μg) | Iron (mg) | Mag-nesium (mg) | Zinc (mg) |
|---|---|---|---|---|---|---|---|---|---|---|---|---|
| Infants | 0.0-0.5 | 5 | 0.4 | 0.3 | 0.3 | 0.3 | 360 | 240 | 35 | 10 | 60 | 3 |
| | 0.5-1.0 | 8 | 0.6 | 0.5 | 0.4 | 0.3 | 540 | 400 | 45 | 15 | 70 | 5 |
| Children | 1-3 | 9 | 0.8 | 0.7 | 0.6 | 1.0 | 800 | 800 | 60 | 15 | 150 | 10 |
| | 4-6 | 12 | 1.1 | 0.9 | 0.9 | 1.5 | 800 | 800 | 80 | 10 | 200 | 10 |
| | 7-10 | 16 | 1.2 | 1.2 | 1.2 | 2.0 | 800 | 800 | 110 | 10 | 250 | 10 |
| Males | 11-14 | 18 | 1.5 | 1.4 | 1.6 | 3.0 | 1,200 | 1,200 | 130 | 18 | 350 | 15 |
| | 15-18 | 20 | 1.8 | 1.5 | 2.0 | 3.0 | 1,200 | 1,200 | 150 | 18 | 400 | 15 |
| | 19-22 | 20 | 1.8 | 1.5 | 2.0 | 3.0 | 800 | 800 | 140 | 10 | 350 | 15 |
| | 23-50 | 18 | 1.6 | 1.4 | 2.0 | 3.0 | 800 | 800 | 130 | 10 | 350 | 15 |
| | 51+ | 16 | 1.5 | 1.2 | 2.0 | 3.0 | 800 | 800 | 110 | 10 | 350 | 15 |
| Females | 11-14 | 16 | 1.3 | 1.2 | 1.6 | 3.0 | 1,200 | 1,200 | 115 | 18 | 300 | 15 |
| | 15-18 | 14 | 1.4 | 1.1 | 2.0 | 3.0 | 1,200 | 1,200 | 115 | 18 | 300 | 15 |
| | 19-22 | 14 | 1.4 | 1.1 | 2.0 | 3.0 | 800 | 800 | 100 | 18 | 300 | 15 |
| | 23-50 | 13 | 1.2 | 1.0 | 2.0 | 3.0 | 800 | 800 | 100 | 18 | 300 | 15 |
| | 51+ | 12 | 1.1 | 1.0 | 2.0 | 3.0 | 800 | 800 | 80 | 10 | 300 | 15 |
| Pregnant | | +2 | +0.3 | +0.3 | 2.5 | 4.0 | 1,200 | 1,200 | 125 | 18+8 | 450 | 20 |
| Lactating | | +4 | +0.5 | +0.3 | 2.5 | 4.0 | 1,200 | 1,200 | 150 | 18 | 450 | 25 |

1. The allowances are intended to provide for individual variations among most normal persons as they live in the United States under usual environmental stresses. Diets should be based on a variety of common foods in order to provide other nutrients for which human requirements have been less well defined.

2. Kilojoules (kJ) = 4.2 × kcal.

3. Retinol equivalents.

4. Assumed to be all as retinol in milk during the first six months of life. All subsequent intakes are assumed to be half as retinol and half as β-carotene when calculated from international units. As retinol equivalents, three-fourths are as retinol and one-fourth as β-carotene.

5. Total vitamin E activity estimated to be 80 percent as α-tocopherol and 20 percent other tocopherols.

6. The folacin allowances refer to dietary sources as determined by *Lactobacillus casei* assay. Pure forms of folacin may be effective in doses less than one fourth of the recommended dietary allowance.

7. Although allowances are expressed as niacin, it is recognized that on the average 1 mg of niacin is derived from each 60 mg of dietary tryptophan.

8. This increased requirement cannot be met by ordinary diets; therefore, the use of supplemental iron is recommended.

Source: *Recommended Dietary Allowances*, Eighth Revised Edition (Washington: National Academy of Sciences, 1974).

## TABLE D
## World Health Organization Recommended Intakes

| Age | Body weight (kilo-grams) | Energy (1) (kilo-calories) | Energy (1) (mega-joules) | Protein (1, 2) (grams) | Vitamin A (3, 4) (micro-grams) | Vitamin D (5, 6) (micro-grams) | Thiamine (3) (milli-grams) | Ribo-flavine (3) (milli-grams) | Niacin (3) (milli-grams) | Folic acid (5) (micro-grams) | Vitamin B12 (5) (micro-grams) | Ascorbic acid (5) (milli-grams) | Calcium (7) (grams) | Iron (5, 8) (milli-grams) |
|---|---|---|---|---|---|---|---|---|---|---|---|---|---|---|
| **Children** | | | | | | | | | | | | | | |
| <1 | 7.3 | 820 | 3.4 | 14 | 300 | 10.0 | 0.3 | 0.5 | 5.4 | 60 | 0.3 | 20 | 0.5-0.6 | 5-10 |
| 1-3 | 13.4 | 1360 | 5.7 | 16 | 250 | 10.0 | 0.5 | 0.8 | 9.0 | 100 | 0.9 | 20 | 0.4-0.5 | 5-10 |
| 4-6 | 20.2 | 1830 | 7.6 | 20 | 300 | 10.0 | 0.7 | 1.1 | 12.1 | 100 | 1.5 | 20 | 0.4-0.5 | 5-10 |
| 7-9 | 28.1 | 2190 | 9.2 | 25 | 400 | 2.5 | 0.9 | 1.3 | 14.5 | 100 | 1.5 | 20 | 0.4-0.5 | 5-10 |
| **Male adolescents** | | | | | | | | | | | | | | |
| 10-12 | 36.9 | 2600 | 10.9 | 30 | 575 | 2.5 | 1.0 | 1.6 | 17.2 | 100 | 2.0 | 20 | 0.6-0.7 | 5-10 |
| 13-15 | 51.3 | 2900 | 12.1 | 37 | 725 | 2.5 | 1.2 | 1.7 | 19.1 | 200 | 2.0 | 30 | 0.6-0.7 | 9-18 |
| 16-19 | 62.9 | 3070 | 12.8 | 38 | 750 | 2.5 | 1.2 | 1.8 | 20.3 | 200 | 2.0 | 30 | 0.5-0.6 | 5-9 |
| **Female adolescents** | | | | | | | | | | | | | | |
| 10-12 | 38.0 | 2350 | 9.8 | 29 | 575 | 2.5 | 0.9 | 1.4 | 15.5 | 100 | 2.0 | 20 | 0.6-0.7 | 5-10 |
| 13-15 | 49.9 | 2490 | 10.4 | 31 | 725 | 2.5 | 1.0 | 1.5 | 16.4 | 200 | 2.0 | 30 | 0.6-0.7 | 12-24 |
| 16-19 | 54.4 | 2310 | 9.7 | 30 | 750 | 2.5 | 0.9 | 1.4 | 15.2 | 200 | 2.0 | 30 | 0.5-0.6 | 14-28 |
| **Adult man** (moderately active) | 65.0 | 3000 | 12.6 | 37 | 750 | 2.5 | 1.2 | 1.8 | 19.8 | 200 | 2.0 | 30 | 0.4-0.5 | 5-9 |
| **Adult woman** (moderately active) | 55.0 | 2200 | 9.2 | 29 | 750 | 2.5 | 0.9 | 1.3 | 14.5 | 200 | 2.0 | 30 | 0.4-0.5 | 14-28 |
| **Pregnancy** (later half) | | +350 | +1.5 | 38 | 750 | 10.0 | +0.1 | +0.2 | +2.3 | 400 | 3.0 | 50 | 1.0-1.2 | (9) |
| **Lactation** (first 6 months) | | +550 | +2.3 | 46 | 1200 | 10.0 | +0.2 | +0.4 | +3.7 | 300 | 2.5 | 50 | 1.0-1.2 | (9) |

1. Energy and Protein Requirements. Report of a Joint FAO/WHO Expert Group, FAO, Rome, 1972.

2. As egg or milk protein.

3. Requirements of Vitamin A, Thiamine, Riboflavin and Niacin. Report of a Joint FAO/WHO Expert Group, FAO, Rome, 1965.

4. As retinol.

5. Requirements of Ascorbic Acid, Vitamin D, Vitamin $B_{12}$, Folate and Iron. Report of a Joint FAO/WHO Expert Group, FAO, Rome, 1970.

6. As cholecalciferol.

7. Calcium Requirements. Report of a FAO/WHO Expert Group, FAO, Rome, 1961.

8. On each line the lower value applies when over 25 percent of calories in the diet come from animal foods, and the higher value when animal foods represent less than 10 percent of calories.

9. For women whose iron intake throughout life has been at the level recommended in this table, the daily intake of iron during pregnancy and lactation should be the same as that recommended for nonpregnant, nonlactating women of childbearing age. For women whose iron status is not satisfactory at the beginning of pregnancy, the requirement is increased, and in the extreme situation of women with no iron stores, the requirement can probably not be met without supplementation.

Source: R. Passmore et al., *Handbook of Human Nutritional Requirements* (Geneva: WHO, 1974).

## TABLE E
### Canadian Recommended Daily Nutrient Intake

| Age | Sex | Weight (kg) | Height (cm) | Energy[1] (kcal) | (MJ)[2] | Protein (g) | Thiamin (mg) | Niacin (NE)[6] | Riboflavin (mg) | Vitamin B6[7] (mg) | Folate[8] (µg) |
|---|---|---|---|---|---|---|---|---|---|---|---|
| 0-6 mo | Both | 6 | — | kg × 117 | kg × 0.49 | kg × 2.2(2.0)[5] | 0.3 | 5 | 0.4 | 0.3 | 40 |
| 7-11 mo | Both | 9 | — | kg × 108 | kg × 0.45 | kg × 1.4 | 0.5 | 6 | 0.6 | 0.4 | 60 |
| 1-3 yrs | Both | 13 | 90 | 1400 | 5.9 | 22 | 0.7 | 9 | 0.8 | 0.8 | 100 |
| 4-6 yrs | Both | 19 | 110 | 1800 | 7.5 | 27 | 0.9 | 12 | 1.1 | 1.3 | 100 |
| 7-9 yrs | M | 27 | 129 | 2200 | 9.2 | 33 | 1.1 | 14 | 1.3 | 1.6 | 100 |
| 7-9 yrs | F | 27 | 128 | 2000 | 8.4 | 33 | 1.0 | 13 | 1.2 | 1.4 | 100 |
| 10-12 yrs | M | 36 | 144 | 2500 | 10.5 | 41 | 1.2 | 17 | 1.5 | 1.8 | 100 |
| 10-12 yrs | F | 38 | 145 | 2300 | 9.6 | 40 | 1.1 | 15 | 1.4 | 1.5 | 100 |
| 13-15 yrs | M | 51 | 162 | 2800 | 11.7 | 52 | 1.4 | 19 | 1.7 | 2.0 | 200 |
| 13-15 yrs | F | 49 | 159 | 2200 | 9.2 | 43 | 1.1 | 15 | 1.4 | 1.5 | 200 |
| 16-18 yrs | M | 64 | 172 | 3200 | 13.4 | 54 | 1.6 | 21 | 2.0 | 2.0 | 200 |
| 16-18 yrs | F | 54 | 161 | 2100 | 8.8 | 43 | 1.1 | 14 | 1.3 | 1.5 | 200 |
| 19-35 yrs | M | 70 | 176 | 3000 | 12.6 | 56 | 1.5 | 20 | 1.8 | 2.0 | 200 |
| 19-35 yrs | F | 56 | 161 | 2100 | 8.8 | 41 | 1.1 | 14 | 1.3 | 1.5 | 200 |
| 36-50 yrs | M | 70 | 176 | 2700 | 11.3 | 56 | 1.4 | 18 | 1.7 | 2.0 | 200 |
| 36-50 yrs | F | 56 | 161 | 1900 | 7.9 | 41 | 1.0 | 13 | 1.2 | 1.5 | 200 |
| 51+ yrs | M | 70 | 176 | 2300[3] | 9.6[3] | 56 | 1.4 | 18 | 1.7 | 2.0 | 200 |
| 51+ yrs | F | 56 | 161 | 1800[3] | 7.5[3] | 41 | 1.0 | 13 | 1.2 | 1.5 | 200 |
| Pregnancy | | | | +300[4] | 1.3[4] | +20 | +0.2 | +2 | +0.3 | +0.5 | +50 |
| Lactation | | | | +500 | 2.1 | +24 | +0.4 | +7 | +0.6 | +0.6 | +50 |

| Age | Sex | Vitamin B12 (µg) | Vitamin C (mg) | Vitamin A (RE)[10] | Vitamin D (µg cholecalciferol)[11] | Vitamin E (mg d-α-tocopherol) | Calcium (mg) | Phosphorus (mg) | Magnesium (mg) | Iodine (µg) | Iron (mg) | Zinc (mg) |
|---|---|---|---|---|---|---|---|---|---|---|---|---|
| 0-6 mo | Both | 0.3 | 20[9] | 400 | 10 | 3 | 500[13] | 250[13] | 50[13] | 35[13] | 7[13] | 4[13] |
| 7-11 mo | Both | 0.3 | 20 | 400 | 10 | 3 | 500 | 400 | 50 | 50 | 7 | 5 |
| 1-3 yrs | Both | 0.9 | 20 | 400 | 10 | 4 | 500 | 500 | 75 | 70 | 8 | 5 |
| 4-6 yrs | Both | 1.5 | 20 | 500 | 5 | 5 | 500 | 500 | 100 | 90 | 9 | 6 |
| 7-9 yrs | M | 1.5 | 30 | 700 | 2.5[12] | 6 | 700 | 700 | 150 | 110 | 10 | 7 |
| | F | 1.5 | 30 | 700 | 2.5[12] | 6 | 700 | 700 | 150 | 100 | 10 | 7 |
| 10-12 yrs | M | 3.0 | 30 | 800 | 2.5[12] | 7 | 900 | 900 | 175 | 130 | 11 | 8 |
| | F | 3.0 | 30 | 800 | 2.5[12] | 7 | 1000 | 1000 | 200 | 120 | 11 | 9 |
| 13-15 yrs | M | 3.0 | 30 | 1000 | 2.5[12] | 9 | 1200 | 1200 | 250 | 140 | 13 | 10 |
| | F | 3.0 | 30 | 800 | 2.5[12] | 7 | 800 | 800 | 250 | 110 | 14 | 10 |
| 16-18 yrs | M | 3.0 | 30 | 1000 | 2.5[12] | 10 | 1000 | 1000 | 300 | 160 | 14 | 12 |
| | F | 3.0 | 30 | 800 | 2.5[12] | 6 | 700 | 700 | 250 | 110 | 14 | 11 |
| 19-35 yrs | M | 3.0 | 30 | 1000 | 2.5[12] | 9 | 800 | 800 | 300 | 150 | 10 | 10 |
| | F | 3.0 | 30 | 800 | 2.5[12] | 6 | 700 | 700 | 250 | 110 | 14 | 9 |
| 36-50 yrs | M | 3.0 | 30 | 1000 | 2.5[12] | 8 | 800 | 800 | 300 | 140 | 10 | 10 |
| | F | 3.0 | 30 | 800 | 2.5[12] | 6 | 700 | 700 | 250 | 100 | 14 | 9 |
| 51+ yrs | M | 3.0 | 30 | 1000 | 2.5[12] | 8 | 800 | 800 | 300 | 140 | 10 | 10 |
| | F | 3.0 | 30 | 800 | 2.5[12] | 6 | 700 | 700 | 250 | 100 | 9 | +10 |
| Pregnancy | | +1.0 | +20 | +100 | +2.5[12] | +1 | +500 | +500 | +25 | +15 | +1[14] | +3 |
| Lactation | | +0.5 | +30 | +400 | +2.5[12] | +2 | +500 | +500 | +75 | +25 | +1[14] | +7 |

1. Recommendations assume characteristic activity pattern for each age group.
2. Megajoules (10⁶ joules). Calculated from the relation 1 kilocalorie = 4.184 kilojoules and rounded to 1 decimal place.
3. Recommended energy intake for age 66+ years reduced to 2000 kcal (8.4 MJ) for men and 1500 kcal (6.3 MJ) for women.
4. Increased energy intake recommended during 2nd and 3rd trimesters. An increase of 100 kcal (418.4kJ) per day is recommended during the 1st trimester.
5. Recommended protein intake of 2.2 g/kg body wt. for infants age 0-2 mo and 2.0 g/kg body wt. for those age 3-5 mo. Protein recommendation for infants 0-11 mo assumes consumption of breast milk or protein of equivalent quality.
6. 1NE (niacin equivalent) is equal to 1 mg of niacin or 60 mg of tryptophan.
7. Recommendations are based on estimated average daily protein intake of Canadians.
8. Recommendation given in terms of free folate.
9. Considerably higher levels may be prudent for infants during the first week of life to guard against neonatal tyrosinemia.
10. 1RE (retinol equivalent) corresponds to a biological activity in humans equal to 1µg retinol (3.33 IU) or 6 µg β-carotene (10 IU).
11. One µg cholecalciferol is equivalent to 1 µg ergocalciferol (40 IU vitamin D activity).
12. Most older children and adults receive vitamin D from irradiation but 2.5 µg daily is recommended. This intake should be increased to 5.0 µg daily during pregnancy and lactation and for those confined indoors or otherwise deprived of sunlight for extended periods.
13. The intake of breast-fed infants may be less than the recommendation but is considered to be adequate.
14. A recommended total intake of 15 mg daily during pregnancy and lactation assumes the presence of adequate stores of iron. If stores are suspected of being inadequate, additional iron as a supplement is recommended.

Source: Dietary Standard of Canada, Revised (Ottawa: Department of Health and Welfare), 1975.

# Glossary of Nutritional Terms

*B-Complex:* Includes thiamine, riboflavin, niacin, vitamin B6, folic acid, vitamin B12, biotin, pantothenic acid, and choline.

*Calcium:* Essential for bone and tooth formation, blood clotting, and nerve transmission. Deficiency leads to poor growth, rickets, osteoporosis, and convulsions. Excess neither harmful nor beneficial.

*Carbohydrates:* Composed of carbon, hydrogen, and oxygen. Together with fat, carbohydrate is the chief source of energy for most humans. The two chief forms are sugar and starch, both of which are eventually converted to glucose, the form in which energy is utilized in the body. Severe restriction of carbohydrate leads to ketosis, a condition in which the acid-base balance of the body is disturbed.

*Cholesterol:* An essential constituent in synthesis of vitamin D and certain hormones. Cholesterol is manufactured by the liver and is not required in food.

*Enzyme:* Complex proteins that cause or accelerate chemical changes in other substances without themselves being changed. Enzymes such as pepsin, for example, aid in breaking down food so that it can be digested. Most enzymes contain a nonprotein component that is called a *coenzyme* if it is organic or an *activator* if it is a metal ion.

*Essential Fatty Acids* (EFA): The two polyunsaturated fatty acids, linoleic and linolenic acid, cannot be synthesized by the human body and hence are called "essential." A third type, arachidonic acid, often classified as essential, can be formed in the body by conversion from linoleic acid. EFA are essential for health in most mammals, human infants, and, presumably, in human adults. They play a role in the regulation of cholesterol metabolism, are important in the functioning of cells, and are precursors in the production of hormonelike compounds known as prostaglandins. Lack of EFA results in poor growth, lowered fertility, and a variety of other conditions. A deficiency is highly unlikely for anyone on a normal diet because the requirement is very low—about 1 or 2 percent of total calories. A variety of plant foods—nuts, seeds, vegetable oils, margarine—supply large amounts of the EFA. Most other plant foods supply small amounts but in total can make a substantial contribution to satisfying the requirement.

*Fiber:* Dietary fiber is not a simple substance but is composed of several types of carbohydrate—cellulose, hemicellulose, pectin, gums, and mucilages—plus a noncarbohydrate substance, lignin. Fiber occurs only in plant foods. Some plant foods—notably sugar, white bread, and fruit juices—lose virtually all of their fiber in processing.

*Folic Acid:* Aids in the synthesis of nucleic acids and aspartic acid, an amino acid. Deficiency causes gastrointestinal disturbances, red tongue, megaloblastic anemia and other abnormalities in the blood. Excess neither harmful nor beneficial.

*Hormone:* Substance formed chiefly in endocrine glands and which, by traveling through the bloodstream, affects the activity in organs or tissues remote from the originating gland. An example is testosterone, which originates in the testes and promotes the growth of secondary sexual characteristics, such as deepening of the male voice at puberty and development of beard and pubic hair.

*Iodine:* Constituent of thyroid hormones that regulate metabolism. Both deficiency and excess can cause goiter. Severe deficiency in early pregnancy or before conception can lead to cretinism in infants.

*Iron:* Component of hemoglobin, the principal component of red blood cells and of enzymes involved in energy metabolism. Deficiency causes anemia. Excess causes cirrhosis of the liver and impaired glucose tolerance and skin pigmentation.

*Lipids:* Like carbohydrates, lipids are composed of carbon, hydrogen, and oxygen, but they differ importantly in the proportion of these elements and in their molecular structure. Lipids include fats, oils, and sterols (including chole*sterol*). They are insoluble in water but soluble in certain solvents, such as alcohol.

*Magnesium:* Activates enzymes in carbohydrate metabolism, is involved in production of protein, and helps regulate body temperature, the nervous system, and muscle contraction. Deficiency, which is usually found only in alcoholics, leads to weakness, spasms, dizziness, and depression. Excess—as in milk of magnesia, the widely used laxative—causes diarrhea.

*Niacin:* Aids in breaking down sugar, synthesizing fat, and the supplying of oxygen to tissues. A deficiency causes pellagra, a disease characterized by weakness, skin rash, diarrhea, and mental disorientation, now rare in affluent societies. People heavily dependent on maize are apt to suffer from the disease for the niacin is present in the grain as niacytin, a form not available for digestion. An excess of niacin causes burning and tingling on the neck, face, and hands.

*Phosphorus:* Essential for forming and strengthening bones, metabolism of fats and carbohydrates, acid-base balance, and involved in the structure of DNA and RNA, the substances controlling heredity. Deficiency, which is extremely rare, causes weakness and demineralization of bones. Excess may promote osteoporosis (see Chapter 6).

*Protein:* Together with carbohydrates and fat, it is one of the three principal dietary components. Unlike carbohydrates and lipids, protein contains nitrogen in addition to carbon, hydrogen, and oxygen. For a fuller explanation of the role of protein, see Chapter 8.

*Riboflavin (vitamin B2):* Aids in transportation of hydrogen component in carbohydrates, fat, and protein. Deficiency causes cracks at corner of mouth, reddened lips, and lesions on eye. Excess neither harmful nor beneficial.

*Sodium:* Necessary for body water balance, acid-base balance, and nerve function. Deficiency leads to apathy, muscle cramps, and reduced appetite.

*Thiamine (vitamin B1):* Necessary for functioning of nervous system and heart muscles, and for growth, fertility, and lactation. Deficiency results in beriberi, a disease characterized by gastrointestinal disturbances, weakness, enlargement of the heart, emaciation, and eventually death. Rare in affluent countries. Excess neither harmful nor beneficial.

*Trace Elements:* In addition to iron, zinc, and iodine, the essential trace elements are copper, chromium, selenium, manganese, molybdenum, fluorine, and cobalt. (Cobalt is only essential as a constituent of vitamin B12.) Other candidates for essential trace element status in humans are nickel, silicon, vanadium, and tin.

*Vitamins:* Organic substances other than proteins, fats, carbohydrates, and mineral salts, which are vital for normal growth and metabolism. By definition, they must be obtained from the diet. Vitamins generally function as coenzymes in enzymatic systems.

*Vitamin A:* Maintains normal vision in dim light, aids in formation of mucus, and is necessary for normal bone growth. Deficiency leads to night blindness and can progress to total blindness. Deficiency also leads to progressive degeneration of epithelial cells, which form the tissue covering the internal and external surfaces of the body. Excess leads to vomiting, headache, peeling of skin, loss of appetite, and swelling of bones.

*Vitamin B12:* Deficiency causes anemia, neurological disorders, and infertility (see Chapter 2). Excess neither harmful nor beneficial.

*Vitamin C:* Principal function is the formation of collagen, the protein substance in the fibers of connective tissue, bone, and cartilage. Deficiency leads to scurvy, a disease characterized by swollen, bleeding gums, hemorrhages under the skin, swollen joints, failure of wounds to heal, and, in extreme cases, death. Excess may lead to kidney stones.

*Vitamin D:* Promotes growth and mineralization of bones. Increases absorption of calcium. Deficiency causes rickets in children and osteomalacia (adult rickets) in adults. Excess causes vomiting, loss of weight, diarrhea, and kidney damage.

*Vitamin E:* Acts as antioxidant in preventing cell-membrane damage. Deficiency, which is extremely rare, may possibly lead to anemia. Excess is believed to be relatively nontoxic.

*Zinc:* Component of enzymes involved in digestion. Mild deficiency can retard wound healing. Severe deficiency can lead to retarded growth and retarded sexual development. Excess causes nausea, vomiting, diarrhea, and fever.

# Recommended Vegetarian Cookbooks

This listing includes only books that are generally available from any well-stocked bookstore.

*Bean Cuisine* by Beverly White (Boston: Beacon Press, 1977). Best source for bean recipes.

*The Book of Tofu* by William Shurtleff and Akiko Aoyagi (Kanagawa-Ken, Japan: Autumn Press, 1975). Printed and distributed in the United States. The comprehensive work on tofu making.

*Chinese Vegetarian Cooking* by Kenneth H. C. Lo (New York: Pantheon Books, 1974).

*Diet for a Small Planet* by Frances Moore Lappé (New York: Ballantine Books, 1971). Overemphasizes "protein complementarity" but has many useful recipes.

*The Farm Vegetarian Cookbook*, edited by Louise Dotzler (Summertown, Tenn.: The Book Publishing Company, 1975). Excellent no-nonsense approach to vegan cooking.

*International Vegetarian Cookery* by Sonya Richmond (New York: Arco, 1965).

*Modern Vegetarian Cookery* by Walter and Jenny Fliess (Baltimore: Penguin Books, 1964).

*Recipes For A Small Planet* by Ellen Buchman Ewald (New York: Ballantine Books, 1973). See comment on *Diet for a Small Planet.*

*Tassajara Cooking* by Edward Espe Brown (Berkeley: Shambhala, 1973). Good on cooking fundamentals.

*The Vegetarian Epicure* by Anna Thomas (New York: Vintage Books, 1972). Well organized and fairly easy to follow.

British readers may find the following useful:

*500 Recipes: Vegetarian Cookery* by Patty Fisher (London: Hamlyn, 1969).

*What's Cooking* by Eva Batt (Middlesex, England: The Vegan Society, 1973). Excellent source of vegan recipes.

# Principal Sources of Calcium, Iron, Vitamin B12, and Sodium in Vegetarian Foods

The tables that follow deal with four nutrients that may, under some circumstances, be a problem for vegetarians—calcium, iron, vitamin B12, and sodium. Insufficient iron and excessive sodium may also, of course, be problem nutrients for omnivores. Calcium may be a problem nutrient for vegans while B12 may be a problem for both vegans and lacto-vegetarians.

## Good Sources of Calcium in Vegetarian Foods
### Ranked by Amount in Average Serving

| | Serving | Calcium (mg) | Calories | Calcium in 100 Calories (mg) |
|---|---|---|---|---|
| Parmesan cheese, grated | 1 ounce (4 tbs) | 390 | 129 | 302 |
| Collards, leaves, no stems | 1 cup cooked | 357* | 63 | 567 |
| Sesame seeds, whole† | 1 ounce | 330 | 160 | 206 |
| Skim milk | 1 cup | 296 | 88 | 336 |
| Yogurt, plain | 1 cup | 294 | 123 | 239 |
| Whole milk | 1 cup | 288 | 159 | 181 |
| Gruyère cheese | 1 ounce | 287 | 117 | 245 |
| Buttermilk | 1 cup | 285 | 99 | 288 |
| Swiss cheese | 1 ounce | 272 | 107 | 254 |
| Carrageenan (Irish moss) | 1 ounce | 252 | — | — |
| Provolone cheese | 1 ounce | 214 | 100 | 214 |
| Edam cheese | 1 ounce | 207 | 101 | 205 |
| Kale, leaves, no stems | 1 cup cooked | 206* | 43 | 479 |
| Cheddar cheese | 1 ounce | 204 | 114 | 179 |
| Muenster cheese | 1 ounce | 203 | 104 | 195 |
| Tilsit cheese | 1 ounce | 198 | 96 | 206 |
| Gouda cheese | 1 ounce | 198 | 101 | 196 |
| Cottage cheese, creamed | 1 cup | 197 | 223 | 88 |
| Colby cheese | 1 ounce | 194 | 112 | 173 |
| Mustard greens, leaves, no stems | 1 cup cooked | 193* | 32 | 603 |
| Brick cheese, caraway cheese | 1 ounce | 191 | 105 | 182 |
| Roquefort cheese | 1 ounce | 188 | 105 | 174 |
| Port du Salut cheese | 1 ounce | 184 | 100 | 184 |
| Pasteurized process cheese | 1 ounce | 174 | 106 | 164 |
| Mozzarella cheese, low moisture | 1 ounce | 163 | 90 | 181 |
| Pasteurized process cheese food | 1 ounce | 163 | 93 | 175 |
| Fortified soy milk (typical values) | 1 cup | 150–160 | 135–160 | 94–119 |
| Blue cheese | 1 ounce | 150 | 100 | 150 |
| Pasteurized process cheese spread | 1 ounce | 159 | 82 | 194 |
| Limburger cheese | 1 ounce | 141 | 93 | 152 |
| Blackstrap molasses | 1 tb | 137 | 43 | 319 |
| Broccoli, stalks, cut | 1 cup cooked | 136* | 40 | 340 |
| Cottage cheese, uncreamed | 1 cup | 131 | 125 | 105 |

| | Serving | Calcium (mg) | Calories | Calcium in 100 Calories (mg) |
|---|---|---|---|---|
| Soybeans | 1 cup cooked | 131 | 234 | 56 |
| Figs, dried | 3½ ounces | 126 | 274 | 46 |
| Sour cream | ½ cup | 112 | 208 | 54 |
| Camembert cheese | 1 ounce | 110 | 85 | 129 |
| Sherbet, orange | 1 cup | 103 | 260 | 40 |
| Rutabaga, sliced | 1 cup cooked | 100 | 60 | 167 |
| Ice milk | ½ cup | 102 | 65 | 157 |
| Okra | 10 pods, cooked | 96* | 31 | 316 |
| Ice cream | ½ cup | 97 | 129 | 75 |
| Pea (navy) beans | 1 cup cooked | 95 | 224 | 42 |
| Great Northern beans | 1 cup cooked | 90 | 212 | 42 |
| Turnips, mashed | 1 cup cooked | 81 | 53 | 153 |
| Lima beans, immature | 1 cup cooked | 98* | 189 | 42 |
| Ricotta cheese made from part skim milk | 1 ounce | 77 | 39 | 197 |
| Parsnips, diced | 1 cup cooked | 70 | 102 | 69 |
| Kidney beans | 1 cup cooked | 70 | 218 | 32 |
| Almonds, shelled | 1 ounce | 66 | 170 | 39 |
| Cabbage | 1 cup cooked | 64 | 29 | 221 |
| Waxed yellow beans or snap beans | 1 cup cooked | 63* | 30 | 210 |
| Artichoke | 1 medium, cooked | 61 | 32 | 191 |
| Summer squash, mashed | 1 cup cooked | 60 | 34 | 176 |
| Filberts (hazelnuts) | 1 ounce shelled | 59 | 180 | 33 |
| Molasses, medium | 1 tb | 58 | 46 | 126 |
| Winter squash, mashed | 1 cup cooked | 57 | 129 | 44 |

|  | Serving | Calcium (mg) | Calories | Calcium in 100 Calories (mg) |
|---|---|---|---|---|
| Lima beans, mature | 1 cup cooked | 55 | 262 | 21 |
| Orange | 2⅝-inch diameter | 54 | 64 | 84 |
| Brazil nuts, shelled | 1 ounce | 53 | 185 | 29 |
| Brie cheese | 1 ounce | 52 | 95 | 55 |
| Carrots, sliced | 1 cup cooked | 51 | 48 | 106 |
| Lentils | 1 cup cooked | 50 | 212 | 24 |

* The calcium values are for fresh vegetables. In some cases the values for frozen vegetables may be considerably lower. One widely distributed brand of frozen broccoli, for example, has only one-fifth the calcium content of fresh broccoli.

† Decorticated sesame seeds contain only 31 mg. calcium per ounce.

Notes:  Most other common vegetarian foods have small amounts of calcium (less than 50 mg.) in amounts usually served. Exceptions are some brands of food yeast, which may supply up to 150 mg. per tablespoon, and large salads made with cos (romaine) or loose-leaf lettuce, endive, or escarole. Per cup shredded, these types of leafy greens supply about 40 mg. of calcium. Iceberg and Bibb lettuce supply considerably less calcium.

Some foods, including spinach, Swiss chard, beet greens, and rhubarb contain substantial calcium but most is bound by oxalic acid present in the vegetables and so cannot be absorbed.

TABLE G
**Good Sources of Iron in Vegetarian Foods**
**Ranked by Amount in Average Serving**

| | Serving | Iron (mg) | Calories | Iron in 100 Calories (mg) |
|---|---|---|---|---|
| Prune juice | 6 ounces | 7.9 | 148 | 5.3 |
| Lima beans, mature, dry | 1 cup cooked | 5.9 | 262 | 2.3 |
| Pea (navy) beans | 1 cup cooked | 5.1 | 224 | 2.3 |
| Great Northern beans | 1 cup cooked | 4.9 | 212 | 2.3 |
| Soybeans | 1 cup cooked | 4.9 | 234 | 2.1 |
| Farina, enriched, cooked with milk | 1 cup cooked | 4.5 | 220 | 2.1 |
| Kidney beans | 1 cup cooked | 4.4 | 218 | 2.0 |
| Lima beans, immature | 1 cup cooked | 4.3 | 189 | 2.3 |
| Lentils | 1 cup cooked | 4.2 | 212 | 2.0 |
| Spinach† | 1 cup cooked | 4.0 | 41 | 9.8 |
| Prunes, no sugar added | 1 cup cooked | 3.8 | 253 | 1.5 |
| Black-eyed peas (cowpeas) | 1 cup cooked | 3.5 | 178 | 2.0 |
| Split peas | 1 cup cooked | 3.4 | 230 | 1.5 |
| Blackstrap molasses | 1 tb | 3.2 | 43 | 7.4 |
| Pumpkin seeds | 1 ounce | 3.2 | 157 | 2.0 |
| Figs, dried | 3½ ounces | 3.0 | 274 | 1.1 |
| Sweet peas | 1 cup cooked | 2.9 | 114 | 2.5 |
| Swiss chard*† | 1 cup cooked | 2.6 | 26 | 10.0 |
| Mustard greens* | 1 cup cooked | 2.5 | 32 | 7.8 |
| Raisins | ½ cup | 2.5 | 210 | 1.2 |
| Dates, moisturized | 10 average | 2.4 | 219 | 1.1 |

| | Serving | Iron (mg) | Calories | Iron in 100 Calories (mg) |
|---|---|---|---|---|
| Watermelon, edible portion | 1 pound | 2.3 | 118 | 1.9 |
| Pistachio nuts, shelled | 1 ounce | 2.1 | 168 | 1.3 |
| Soy milk, fortified (typical values) | 1 cup | 2.0–3.7 | 135–160 | 1.5–2.3 |
| Sunflower seeds, hulled | 1 ounce | 2.0 | 159 | 1.3 |
| Apricots, dried | 5 medium | 1.9 | 91 | 2.1 |
| Kale* | 1 cup cooked | 1.8 | 43 | 4.2 |
| White rice, enriched | 1 cup cooked | 1.8 | 223 | .8 |
| Black walnuts, shelled | 1 ounce | 1.7 | 178 | 1.0 |
| Torula yeast | 1 tb | 1.6 | 23 | 7.0 |
| Tomato juice | 6 ounces | 1.6 | 35 | 4.6 |
| Whole-wheat bread | 2 slices | 1.6 | 122 | 1.3 |
| Winter squash | 1 cup cooked | 1.6 | 129 | 1.2 |
| Collards* | 1 cup cooked | 1.5 | 63 | 2.3 |
| Strawberries | 1 cup | 1.5 | 55 | 2.7 |
| Blueberries | 1 cup | 1.5 | 90 | 1.7 |
| Brewer's yeast | 1 tb | 1.4 | 23 | 6.1 |
| Oatmeal | 1 cup cooked | 1.4 | 132 | 1.1 |
| White bread, enriched | 2 slices | 1.4 | 152 | .9 |
| Converted rice | 1 cup cooked | 1.4 | 186 | .8 |
| Pasta products | 1 cup cooked | 1.4 | 200 | .7 |
| Artichoke | 1 medium | 1.3 | 32 | 4.1 |
| Blackberries | 1 cup | 1.3 | 84 | 1.5 |
| Parsnips, mashed | 1 cup cooked | 1.3 | 139 | .9 |
| Almonds, shelled | 1 ounce | 1.3 | 170 | .8 |
| Eggplant, sliced | 1 cup | 1.2 | 38 | 3.2 |
| Broccoli* | 1 cup | 1.2 | 40 | 3.0 |
| Molasses, medium extraction | 1 tb | 1.2 | 46 | 2.6 |
| Egg‡ | 1 large | 1.2 | 82 | 1.5 |
| Lettuce, Bibb, Boston | 1 cup | 1.1 | 8 | 13.8 |
| Raspberries, red | 1 cup | 1.1 | 70 | 1.6 |
| Melons, cantaloupe, 5-inch diameter | ½ | 1.1 | 82 | 1.3 |
| Apple juice | 6 ounces | 1.1 | 87 | 1.3 |
| Potato, baked | 1 7-ounce | 1.1 | 145 | .8 |

|  | Serving | Iron (mg) | Calories | Iron in 100 Calories (mg) |
|---|---|---|---|---|
| Summer squash, mashed | 1 cup cooked | 1.0 | 34 | 2.9 |
| Sweet potato, baked | 1 5-ounce | 1.0 | 161 | .6 |
| Cashew nuts, shelled | 1 ounce | 1.1 | 159 | .7 |
| Corn | 1 cup cooked | 1.0 | 137 | .7 |
| Brazil nuts, shelled | 1 ounce | 1.0 | 185 | .5 |
| Brown rice | 1 cup cooked | 1.0 | 232 | .4 |
| Filberts (hazelnuts), shelled | 1 ounce | 1.0 | 180 | .6 |

* The iron values are for fresh vegetables. In some cases, the values for frozen vegetables may be considerably lower. One widely distributed brand of frozen broccoli, for example, has only one-fifth the iron content of fresh broccoli.
† Iron may be bound to oxalic acid and so may not be available for absorption.

‡ The iron in egg is more readily absorbed than that from plant foods.

Note: Most other common vegetarian foods have small amounts of iron (less than 1 mg.) in amounts usually served.

## TABLE H
### Sources of Vitamin B12 in Vegetarian Foods
### Ranked by Amount in Average Serving

| | Serving | Vitamin B12 (mcg) | Calories | Vitamin B12 in 100 Calories (mcg) |
|---|---|---|---|---|
| Yogurt, plain | 1 cup | 1.3 | 123 | 1.1 |
| Cottage cheese, creamed | 1 cup | 1.3 | 223 | .6 |
| Cottage cheese, uncreamed | 1 cup | 1.2 | 125 | 1.0 |
| Yogurt, flavored | 1 cup | 1–1.2 | 225 | .4–.5 |
| Egg | 1 large | 1.0 | 82 | 1.2 |
| Skim milk | 1 cup | .9 | 88 | 1.0 |
| Whole milk | 1 cup | .9 | 159 | .6 |
| Ice milk | 1 cup | .9 | 199 | .5 |
| Tilsit cheese | 1 ounce | .6 | 96 | .6 |
| Ice cream | 1 cup | .6 | 257 | .2 |
| Brie cheese | 1 ounce | .5 | 95 | .5 |
| Buttermilk | 1 cup | .5 | 99 | .5 |
| Swiss cheese | 1 ounce | .5 | 107 | .5 |
| Gruyère cheese | 1 ounce | .5 | 117 | .4 |
| Camembert cheese | 1 ounce | .4 | 85 | .5 |
| Port du Salut cheese | 1 ounce | .4 | 100 | .4 |
| Provolone cheese | 1 ounce | .4 | 100 | .4 |
| Edam cheese | 1 ounce | .4 | 101 | .4 |
| Muenster cheese | 1 ounce | .4 | 104 | .4 |
| Brick cheese | 1 ounce | .4 | 105 | .4 |
| Soy milk, fortified (typical values) | 1 cup | .3–.5 | 135–160 | .2–.3 |
| Pasteurized process cheese food | 1 ounce | .3 | 90 | .3 |
| Limburger cheese | 1 ounce | .3 | 93 | .3 |
| Blue cheese | 1 ounce | .3 | 104 | .3 |
| Mozzarella cheese, low moisture | 1 ounce | .2 | 90 | .2 |
| Pasteurized process cheese | 1 ounce | .2 | 106 | .2 |
| Roquefort cheese | 1 ounce | .2 | 105 | .2 |
| Colby cheese | 1 ounce | .2 | 112 | .2 |
| Cheddar cheese | 1 ounce | .2 | 114 | .2 |
| Sherbet, orange | 1 cup | .2 | 260 | .1 |
| Pasteurized process cheese spread | 1 ounce | .1 | 82 | .1 |
| Cream cheese | 1 ounce | .1 | 99 | .1 |
| Caraway cheese | 1 ounce | .1 | 107 | .1 |
| Neufchatel cheese | 1 ounce | .1 | 74 | .1 |

TABLE I
## Vegetarian Foods High in Sodium
### Ranked by Amount in Average Portions

|  | Serving | Sodium (mg) |
|---|---|---|
| Self-rising flour, unsifted | 1 cup | 1350 |
| Soy sauce | 1 tb | 1320 |
| Bread stuffing mix, moistened | 1 cup | 1260 |
| Soup, canned | 1 cup | 840–1050 |
| Beans canned in tomato or molasses sauce | 1 cup cooked | 1070 |
| Soup made from dry mix | 1 cup | 690–1025 |
| Baking soda | 1 tb | 1000 |
| Pickles | 1 medium (2 ounces) | 930 |
| Green olives | 10 large | 925 |
| Cottage cheese, creamed and low-fat* | 1 cup | 850–920 |
| Corn, cream style, canned | 1 cup cooked | 604 |
| Asparagus, canned | 1 cup cooked | 570 |
| Potatoes, mashed, made from dehydrated flakes | 1 cup cooked | 490–540 |
| Parmesan cheese, grated | 1 ounce | 430 |
| Fruit pies, 9-inch-diameter, store-bought | 1/8 sector | 180–530 |
| Spinach, canned | 1 cup cooked | 490 |
| Tomato, vegetable juice | 1 cup | 485 |
| Pretzels | 1 ounce | 475 |
| Pancakes made from mix | 3 1-ounce cakes | 450 |
| Cakes, store-bought | 3½ ounces | 110–450 |
| Cheese pizza, 15-ounce, 10-inch-diameter | 1/6 sector | 430 |
| Pasteurized process cheese | 1 ounce | 405 |
| Lima beans and peas, canned | 1 cup cooked | 400 |
| Blue cheese | 1 ounce | 395 |
| Olives, ripe | 10 large | 385 |
| Corn, whole kernel, canned | 1 cup cooked | 385 |
| Pasteurized process cheese spread | 1 ounce | 380 |
| Ready-to-eat breakfast cereals | 1 cup | 150–385 |
| Beets, canned | 1 cup | 380 |
| Carrots, canned | 1 cup cooked | 365 |
| Baking powder | 1 teaspoon | up to 350 |
| Potato sticks | 1 cup | up to 350 |
| Romano cheese | 1 ounce | 340 |
| Pasteurized process cheese food | 1 ounce | 335 |
| Buttermilk | 1 cup | 320 |
| Pudding from prepared mix | 1 cup | 320 |

| | Serving | Sodium (mg) |
|---|---|---|
| Tomatoes, canned | 1 cup | 315 |
| Crackers, store-bought | 1 ounce | 85–310 |
| Snap, wax beans, canned | 1 cup cooked | 305 |
| Ricotta cheese | 1 cup | 305 |
| Edam and American cold pack cheese | 1 ounce | 275 |
| Biscuits made from mix | 1 ounce | 270 |
| Rolls and buns, store-bought | 1½ ounces | 165–265 |
| Camembert, Gouda, Limberger, provolone and Tilsit cheese | 1 ounce | 200–249 |
| Lima beans, baby, canned | 1 cup cooked | 230 |
| Waffle, frozen | 1 ounce | 220 |
| Most store-bought salad dressings† | 1 tb | 110–220 |
| Muffin made from mix | 1½ ounces | 210 |
| Peanut butter, salt added | 1 ounce (2 tbs) | 200 |
| Potato chips | 10 chips | up to 200 |
| Brick, Brie, caraway, cheddar, Cheshire, Colby, Monterey, Muenster, Port du Salut | 1 ounce | 150–199 |
| Peas, frozen | 1 cup cooked | 185 |
| Lima beans, Fordhook, frozen | 1 cup cooked | 170 |
| Cookies | 1 ounce | up to 160 |
| Yogurt, plain and flavored | 8 ounces | 120–160 |
| Catsup | 1 tb | 155 |
| Bread, whole-wheat, white, cracked-wheat, rye, store-bought | 1 slice | 115–150 |
| Milk, whole or skim | 1 cup | 125 |
| Peanuts, roasted, salted, shelled | 1 ounce | 120 |
| Sweet potatoes, canned | 1 cup cooked | 95–120 |
| Mozzarella and Neufchatel cheese | 1 ounce | 115 |
| Spinach, frozen | 1 cup cooked | 105 |

* Unless salted, uncreamed cottage cheese has little sodium (under 20 milligrams per cup). Rinsing of the creamed product in a colander removes most of the sodium.

† Mayonnaise and mayonnaise-type salad dressings have about 85 milligrams of sodium per ounce.

Note: Swiss, Roquefort, Gruyère and cream cheese are the only widely used cheeses that have less than 100 milligrams sodium per ounce.

Sources for data in Appendix 6: Catherine F. Adams, *Nutritive Value of American Foods*, Agriculture Handbook No. 456 (Washington, D.C.: United States Department of Agriculture, 1975; "Composition and Nutritive Value of Dairy Foods," *Dairy Council Digest*, 47:26, 1976; Martha Louise Orr, *Pantothenic Acid, Vitamin B6, and Vitamin B12 in Foods*, Home Economics Research Report No. 36 (Washington: U.S. Department of Agriculture, 1969).

# Sources

## General

The source for most of the statements regarding general nutrition are from *Modern Nutrition in Health and Disease*, Fifth Edition, Robert S. Goodhart and Maurice E. Shils, editors (Philadelphia: Lea & Febiger, 1973), or from *Human Nutrition and Dietetics*, Sixth Edition, by Sir Stanley Davidson et al. (Edinburgh: Churchill Livingston, 1975). *Modern Nutrition* is the most authoritative American text, while *Human Nutrition* is the most authoritative British text. *Present Knowledge in Nutrition*, Fourth Edition, D. M. Hegsted et al., editors (New York: The Nutrition Foundation, 1976) is a most useful supplement to these two standard works. The two official sources on dietary allowances referred to in the text are *Recommended Dietary Allowances*, Eighth Revised Edition (Washington: National Academy of Sciences, 1974) and *Handbook of Human Nutritional Requirements* by R. Passmore et al. (Geneva: World Health Organization, 1974). Sources for nutrient composition are *Composition of Foods*, Agriculture Handbook No. 8 (Washington: United

States Department of Agriculture, 1963), *Nutritive Value of American Foods*, Agriculture Handbook No. 456 (Washington: United States Department of Agriculture, 1975), and *Food Consumption Table for Use in East Asia* (Washington: National Institutes of Health—U.S. Department of Health, Education, and Welfare, 1972).

An old yet highly informative review of the literature on vegetarian diets will be found in a series of three articles by Mervyn G. Hardinge and Hulda Crooks in the *Journal of the American Dietetic Association*. Under the general title "Non-flesh dietaries," the series appeared as follows: "1. Historical background," 43:545, 1963; "2. Scientific literature," 43:550, 1963; "3. Adequate and inadequate," 43:537, 1964.

The only comprehensive comparative study of lacto-vegetarians vs. vegans vs. omnivores was made by Mervyn G. Hardinge and Frederick J. Stare. Under the general title "Nutritional studies of vegetarians," it appeared in five installments, as follows, "1. Nutritional, physical and laboratory studies," *J Clin Nutr* 2:73, 1954(A); "2. Dietary and serum levels of cholesterol," *J Clin Nutr* 2:83, 1954(B); "3. Dietary levels of fiber," *Am J Clin Nutr* 6:523, 1958; "4. Dietary fatty acids and serum cholesterol levels," *Am J Clin Nutr* 10:516, 1962; "5. Proteins and essential amino acids," *J Am Diet Assoc* 48:25, 1966.

An excellent review of health statistics for the lacto-vegetarian Seventh Day Adventists will be found in an article by Roland L. Phillips, "Role of life-style and dietary habits in risk of cancer among Seventh Day Adventists," *Cancer Res* 35:3513, 1975. Other articles on the Adventists include: R. O. West and O. B. Hayes, "Diet and serum cholesterol levels—a comparison between vegetarians and non-vegetarians in the Seventh Day Adventist group," *Am J Clin Nutr* 21:853, 1968; E. L. Wynder et al., "Cancer and coronary artery disease among Seventh Day Adventists," *Cancer* 12:1016, 1959; B. K. Armstrong et al., "Hematological, vitamin B12, and folate studies on Seventh Day Adventist vegetarians," *Am J Clin Nutr* 27:712, 1974; and R. T. Walden, "Effect of environment on the serum cholesterol–triglyceride distribution among Seventh Day Adventists," *Am J Med* 36:269, 1964.

Another important group of lacto-vegetarians are the Trappist monks. Information on the Trappists will be found in "The influence of nutrition and ways of life on blood cholesterol and the prevalence of hypertension and coronary heart disease among Trappist and Benedictine monks," by J. J. Groen et al., *Am J Clin Nutr* 10:456, 1962. Other reports on the Trappists are by E. P. McCullagh and L. A. Lewis, "A study of diet, blood lipids and vascular disease in Trappist monks," *New Engl J Med* 263:569, 1960; J. G. Barrow et al., "Studies in atherosclerosis. III. An epidemiologic study of atherosclerosis in Trappist and Benedictine monks," *Ann Intern Med* 52:368, 1960; C. A. Cacerces et al., "An evaluation of clinical and laboratory findings in male subjects on long term, low fat, low protein diets," *New Engl J Med* 269:550, 1963; J. B. Calatayud et al., "Long term, low fat, low protein diets and their effect on normal

Trappist subjects," *Am J Clin Nutr* 12:368, 1963.

Reviews of the literature on vegan diets have been published in *Plant Foods for Human Nutrition*, as follows: A. N. Kurtha and F. R. Ellis, "The nutritional, clinical and economic aspects of vegan diets," 2:13, 1970; F. R. Ellis and V. M. E. Montegriffo, "The health of vegans," 2:93, 1971; D. S. Miller and P. Mumford, "The nutritive value of Western vegan and vegetarian diets," 2:201, 1972. A review by F. R. Ellis and P. Mumford, "The nutritional status of vegans and vegetarians," will be found in *Proc Nutr Soc* 26:205, 1967.

Perhaps the most intensive study of veganism to date has been made by T. A. B. Sanders in his doctoral thesis, *The Composition of Red Cell Lipid and Adipose Tissue in Vegans, Vegetarians and Omnivores* (University of London, 1977). Much of the same ground is covered in T. A. B. Sanders et al., "Studies of vegans: the fatty acid composition of plasma choline phosphoglycerides, erythrocytes, adipose tissue, and breast milk, and some indicators of susceptibility to ischemic heart disease in vegans and omnivore controls," *Am J Clin Nutr* 31:805, 1978. Other studies of vegans include K. T. Lee et al., "Geographic studies of atherosclerosis," *Arch Environ Health* 4:10, 1962; F. R. Ellis et al., "The health of vegans compared with omnivores. Assessment by health questionnaire," *Plant Foods for Man* 2:43, 1976; F. R. Ellis and V. M. E. Montegriffo, "Veganism, clinical findings and Investigations," *Am J Clin Nutr* 23:249, 1970; V. C. Aries et al., "The effect of a strict vegetarian diet on the faecal flora and faecal steroid concentration," *J Pathol* 103:54, 1971.

# CHAPTER 1: A STRATEGY FOR VEGETARIAN NUTRITION

Information on health during wartime will be found in M. Hindehede, "The effect of food restriction during war on mortality in Copenhagen," *JAMA* 20:381, 1920; A. Strom and R. A. Jensen, "Mortality from circulatory diseases in Norway, 1940–1945," *Lancet* 1:126, 1951; H. E. Magee, "Application of nutrition to public health," *Br Med J* 1:475, 1946; H. E. Schornagel, "The connection between nutrition and mortality from coronary sclerosis during and after World War II," *Docu Med Geog Trop* 4:173, 1952; H. Malmros, "The relation of nutrition to health," *Act Med Scand* suppl. 246:137, 1950; and R. H. Daw, letter, *Lancet* 1:1079, 1954.

Articles on dietary fiber abound. One of the most readable is "Dietary fiber and disease," *JAMA* 229:1068, 1974, by D. P. Burkitt and N. S. Painter, two of the leading advocates of the fiber theory. The most comprehensive statement of the theory will be found in *Refined Carbohydrates and Disease*, D. P. Burkitt and H. C. Trowell, editors (New

York: Academic Press, 1975). Three perceptive appraisals of the theory are by J. H. Cummings in his "Progress report—dietary fibre" in *Gut* 14:69, 1973; by A. I. Mendeloff in *Present Knowledge in Nutrition*, Fourth Edition (New York: The Nutrition Foundation, 1976), p. 392; and A. I. Mendeloff, "Dietary fiber and human health," *New Engl J Med* 297:811, 1977. Anyone interested in the chemistry of dietary fiber will find D. A. T. Southgate's "Fibre in nutrition," *Bibtheca Nutr Dieta* 22:109, 1975, of value. See also D. A. T. Southgate et al., "A guide to calculating intakes of dietary fiber," *J Human Nutr* 30:303, 1976. The data on fiber consumption by lacto-vegetarians and vegans is from Hardinge and Stare, 1958, op. cit.

The case against sugar as a cause of major disease is put forward in several articles by John Yudkin: "Evolutionary and historical changes in dietary carbohydrates," *Am J Clin Nutr* 20:108, 1967; "Why blame sugar?" *Chem Ind*, September 2, 1967; "Diet and coronary thrombosis," *Lancet* 2:155, 1957; "Sucrose and cardiovascular disease," *Proc Nutr Soc* 31:331, 1972; "Sucrose and heart disease," *Nutr Today*, Spring 1969, p. 16; "Sugar intake and myocardial infarction," *Am J Clin Nutr* 20:503, 1967; "Patterns and trends in carbohydrate consumption and their relation to disease," *Proc Nutr Soc* 23:149, 1964. Professor Yudkin's theories are also presented in his popular and highly readable book *Sweet and Dangerous* (New York: Bantam, 1973).

The possibility that sugar may be a cause of obesity is discussed in Yudkin's book and also in H. F. Sassoon, "Time factors in obesity," *Am J Clin Nutr* 26:776, 1973. The recent work on monkeys and sugar was reported by G. S. Berenson et al. in *Circulation* 56: III-242, 1977, and in a transcript of Berenson's talk at the American Heart Association Science Writers Forum, Newport Beach, California, January 17, 1978, "Synergistic effects of dietary sodium and sucrose on induction of hypertension in spider monkeys." The study on sugar and kidney damage is from S. S. Kang et al., "Renal damage in rats caused by dietary sucrose," *Biochem Soc Trans* 5:235, 1977.

Informative reviews of the latest medical thinking on heart disease will be found in H. C. McGill and G. E. Mott, "Diet and coronary heart disease," in *Present Knowledge*, p. 376, and in D. Kritchevsky, "Diet and atherosclerosis," *Am J Pathol* 84:615, 1976. A detailed discussion of the complexities in cardiovascular research will be found in a series of articles by G. N. Kolata and J. L. Marx in *Science* 194: 509, 592, 711, 821, and 1029 (1976). The views of W. P. Castelli are reported in a transcript of his talk before the American Heart Association Fourth Science Writers Forum, San Antonio, Texas, January 16, 1977. The epidemiological information on coronary heart disease is from H. Blackburn, "Concepts and controversies about the prevention of coronary heart disease" in *Cardiovascular Problems*, Henry I. Russek, editor (Baltimore: University Park Press, 1976), p. 123.

The views of E. H. Ahrens were reported in the *New York Times*,

September 4, 1977, p. 1. For an interesting and provocative argument regarding the relationship of diet to heart disease, see G. V. Man, "Diet-heart: end of an era," *New Engl J Med* 297:644, 1977.

The discussion of fat and cancer is based on the November 1975 issue of *Cancer Research* (the entire issue is devoted to papers on nutrition and cancer); M. E. Shils, "Nutrition and cancer: dietary deficiency and modifications," in *Cancer Epidemiology and Prevention*, David Schottenfeld, editor (Springfield, Ill.: Charles C Thomas, 1975), p. 153; and the *Dairy Council Digest*, 4:25, 1975. Ernest L. Wynder's remark regarding nutrition and cancer is from his "Introductory remarks" in *Cancer Research* 35:3238, 1975.

The American Heart Association recommendations will be found in the society's pamphlet, *Diet and Coronary Heart Disease* (New York: 1973). Those of the Royal College of Physicians will be found in *J Roy Coll Phys* 10:213, 1976; those of the Scandinavians will be found in *Human Nutrition*, p. 652; while those for Italy and the U.S.S.R. will be found in "Tables of recommended nutrient intakes in different European countries," *Nutr Metab* 21:251, 1977. The views of W. E. and S. L. Conners will be found in "The key role of nutritional factors in the prevention of coronary heart disease," *Prev Med* 1:49, 1972. The position of the Longevity Foundation of America is set forth in *Live Longer Now* by Jon Leonard, J. L. Hofer, and N. Pritikin (New York: Grosset & Dunlap, 1974). The reference to the Hos tribe is from *Human Nutrition and Dietetics*, p. 89. Dr. E. L. Wynder's guideline for fat is in "The epidemiology of cancer of the large bowel," *Digestive Dis* 19:937, 1974.

The possibility that caffeine may contribute to hypertension was reported in D. Robertson et al., "Effects of caffeine on plasma renin activity, catecholamines and blood pressure," *New Engl J Med* 298:181, 1978.

The new information on eggs and blood cholesterol is reported in M. W. Porter et al., "Effect of dietary egg on serum cholesterol and triglycerides in human males," *Am J Clin Nutr* 30:490, 1977; G. Slater et al., "Plasma cholesterol and triglycerides in men with added eggs in the diet," *Nutr Rpts Internatl* 14:249, 1976; and F. A. Kummerow et al., "The influence of egg consumption on the serum cholesterol level in human subjects," *Am J Clin Nutr* 30:664, 1977. The comment on eggs by Briggs and Weinberger is from "Nutrition update, 1977," *J Nutr Educ* 9:173, 1977. The new information on egg consumption and blood cholesterol has by no means ended the controversy over dietary cholesterol. For two opposing views, see C. J. Glueck and W. E. Conner, "Diet-coronary heart disease relationships reconnoitered" *Am J Clin Nutr* 31:727, 1978, and R. Reiser, "Oversimplification of diet: coronary heart disease relationships and exaggerated diet recommendations," *Am J Clin Nutr* 31:865, 1978.

Dr. Altschule's views on cholesterol are from "The cholesterol problem," *Medical Counterpoint*, January 1970, p. 11.

The large-scale study by R. L. Philips et al., "Coronary heart mortality among Seventh Day Adventists with differing dietary habits: a preliminary report" appeared in *Am J Clin Nutr* 31:S191, 1978.

Information on the blood cholesterol level of vegans will be found in Hardinge and Stare 1954(B), op. cit.; Lee, 1962, op. cit.; Ellis and Montegriffo, 1970, op. cit.; Ellis and Mumford, 1967, op. cit.; Sanders, 1977, op. cit.; Sanders et al., 1978, op. cit.; and Sacks, 1975, op. cit. Information on blood cholesterol of lacto-vegetarians will be found in Hardinge, 1954(B), op. cit.; West, 1968, op. cit.; Walden, 1964, op. cit.; Groen, 1962, op. cit.; McCullagh, 1960, op. cit.; Barrow, 1960, op. cit. The possible association of vegetable protein with lower blood cholesterol is reported in Carrol, "Dietary protein in relation to plasma cholesterol levels and atherosclerosis," *Nutr Rev* 36:1, 1978.

Information on leanness of vegans will be found in Sanders, 1977, op. cit.; Sanders et al., 1978, op. cit.; Hardinge, 1954(A), op. cit.; W. F. Donath et al., "Health, diet and vegetarianism," *Nutr Abst Rev* 23:892, 1953; F. M. Sacks et al., "Plasma lipids in vegetarians and controls," *New Engl J Med* 292:114B, 1975; R. H. Hutcheson et al., "Nutritional Status of a Community of Young Vegans" (Nashville: Tennessee Department of Public Health, undated); and Ellis and Montegriffo, 1970, op. cit. Information on leanness among lacto-vegetarians will be found in B. Armstrong et al., "Blood pressure in Seventh Day Adventist vegetarians," *Am J Epidemiology* 105:444, 1977, and Philips et al., 1978, op. cit.

The hypothesis regarding dietary fiber and weight loss is from K. W. Heaton, "Food fibre as an obstacle to energy intake," *Lancet* 2:1418, 1973. A critical appraisal of the hypothesis is offered by W. P. T. James and J. H. Cummings in "Dietary fibre and energy regulation," *Lancet* 1:61, 1974. A stimulating historical analysis of the subject will be found in H. Trowell's, "Obesity in the Western World," *Plant Foods for Man* 1:157, 1975. Sander's statement regarding vitamin B12 and body fat is from a personal communication.

Information on blood pressure of vegans and near vegans will be found in F. M. Sacks, "Blood pressure in vegetarians and controls," *Am J Epidemial* 100:390, 1974. This study contains many references suggesting a positive corellation between consumption of animal food and blood pressure. Dr. H. P. Haines of Northwick Park Hospital, England, has noted that English vegans have lower blood pressure than English meat eaters (personal communication). Information on the blood pressure of lacto-vegetarians will be found in B. Armstrong et al., 1977, op. cit., and in Philips et al., 1978, op. cit. The information on P/S ratio and blood pressure is from J. N. Iacono, "Reduction in blood pressure associated with high polyunsaturated fat diets that reduce blood cholesterol in man," *Prev Med* 4:426, 1975.

The low cancer rates among Seventh Day Adventists are reported in Philips, 1975, op. cit. The cancer rates among Mormons are reported by J. L. Lyons et al., "Cancer incidence in Mormons and non-Mormons in

Utah, 1966–1970," *New Engl J Med* 294:129, 1976. The long-term study of cancer among Adventists now in progress is described in "Rationale and methods for an epidemiological study of cancer among Seventh Day Adventists—a low risk group" in *Proc Mani Conference on Cancer Registeries*, November 10–14, 1975 (in press).

# CHAPTER 2: VEGETARIAN DIETS FOR ADULTS

The quotation from *Mademoiselle* is from "Vegetarian diets" by J. L. Rodgers in the August 1977 issue, p. 56.

Information on menu plans for lacto-vegetarian diets will be found in *Diet Manual* (Loma Linda, Ca.: Seventh Day Adventist Dietetic Association, 1975). Information on vegan nutrition will be found in a series of articles in *The Vegan*, the official publication of the British Vegan Society. The articles, written by F. R. Ellis and/or T. A. B. Sanders appear as follows: "Vegan nutrition—proteins," Spring 1975; "Vegan nutrition—carbohydrates," Summer 1975; "Vegan nutrition—fats," Autumn 1975; "Vegan nutrition—Vitamins, Part 1," Winter 1975; "Vitamin B12," Spring 1977; "Minerals in the vegan diet," Autumn 1977.

The information on vitamin C, tea, and iron absorption is from D. Derman et al., "Iron absorption from a cereal-based meal containing cane sugar fortified with ascorbic acid," *Br J Nutr* 38:261, 1977.

For information about zinc and vegetarian diets see P. M. Bodzy et al., "Zinc status in the vegetarian," *Fed Proc* 36:1139, 1977; and J. H. Freeland et al., "Trace mineral content of vegetarian foods," *Fed Proc* 36:1139, 1977. F. R. Ellis's comments on the iron and zinc status of vegan diets is from a personal communication.

The statement by the National Academy of Sciences on vegan diets will be found in *JAMA* 233:898, 1975. The information on Korean monks is from Lee, 1962, op. cit. The information on inadequate vegan diets is from Hardinge and Crooks, 1964, op. cit.

The effect of vitamin C on vitamin B12 is from "Destruction of vitamin B12 by ascorbic acid," by V. Herbert and E. Jacobs, *JAMA* 230:241, 1974. The work of Herbert and Jacobs has been disputed by H. L. Newmark et al. in "Stability of vitamin B12 in the presence of ascorbic acid," *Am J Clin Nutr* 29:645, 1976. See also V. Herbert et al., "Destruction of vitamin B12 by vitamin C" (letter), *Am J Clin Nutr* 30:297, 1976, and H. L. Newmark and J. Scheiner, "Destruction of vitamin B12 by vitamin C" (letter), *Am J Clin Nutr* 30:299, 1976.

The vitamin B12 deficiency problem is discussed in several of the review articles on veganism listed above and also in F. Wokes et al., "Human dietary deficiency of vitamin B12," *Am J Clin Nutr* 3:375, 1955; E. P. West and F. R. Ellis, "The electroencephalogram in veganism, vegetarianism, vitamin B12 deficiency, and in controls," *J Neurol Neurosurg Psychiat* 29:391, 1966; F. R. Ellis and F. Wokes, "The treatment of dietary deficiency of vitamin B12 with vegetable protein foods," *Nutritio et Dieta* 9:81, 1967; and A. D. M. Smith, "Veganism: a critical survey with observations on vitamin B12 metabolism," *Lancet* 1:1655, 1962. Information on the B12 content of seaweed is from H. Lundin and L. E. Ericson, "On the occurrence of vitamins in marine algae," in *Proceedings Second International Seaweed Symposium 1955* (New York: Pergamon Press, 1956), p. 39. The comment by Dr. F. R. Ellis on vitamin B12 is from a personal communication.

Dr. T. A. B. Sanders's suggestions regarding polyunsaturated fatty acids is in "Vegan diet—a remedy for diseases of affluence" (in press). See also R. H. Dowling, "The enterohepatic circulation of bile acids as they relate to lipid disorders," *J Clin Path* 26 suppl. (Asso Clin Path) 5:59, 1973; and V. C. Aries et al., "The effect of a strict vegetarian diet on the faecal flora and faecal steroid concentration," *J Path* 103:54, 1971.

The possibility that calcium requirements may be as high as 800 mg. a day is reported in D. H. Marshal et al., "Calcium, phosphorus and magnesium requirement," *Proc Nutr Soc* 35:163, 1976. For information on protein and calcium, see *Present Knowledge*, pp. 234–37.

The reference to possible riboflavin deficiency is from K. Guggenheim et al., "Composition and nutritive value of diets consumed by strict vegetarians," *Br J Nutr* 16:467, 1962. Mayer's experiment on exercise and obesity is discussed in his book *Overweight: Causes, Cost and Control* (Englewood Cliffs, N.J.: Prentice-Hall, 1968).

# CHAPTERS 3 AND 4: VEGETARIAN DIETS FOR INFANTS . . . THROUGH ADOLESCENCE

Basic sources for these chapters are Samuel Foman's *Infant Nutrition*, Second Edition (Philadelphia: W. B. Saunders, 1974); *Nutrition in Preschool and School Age, Symposia of the Swedish Nutrition Foundation VII*, Gunner Blix, editor (Uppsala: Swedish Nutrition Foundation, 1969); *Adolescent Nutrition and Growth*, Felix P. Heald, editor (New York: Appleton-Century-Crofts, 1969); and Margaret McWilliams' *Nutrition for the Growing Years* (New York: John Wiley, 1967). Clara Davis's classic experiment was reported in "Results of self-selection of diets by young children," *Can Med Assoc J*, September 1939, p. 257, and was reprinted in *Child and Family* 10:210, 1971. Advice about the proportion of fat in infant diets is from B. Lindquist, *Nutrition in Preschool and School Age*, op. cit., p. 56.

Information regarding health developments at The Farm are in R. H. Hutcheson et al., op. cit., and in personal communications from H. Lee

Fleshhood and Sara E. Cummings of the Tennessee Department of Health, Dr. J. O. Williams, Jr., of Mount Pleasant, Tennessee, and Margaret Nofziger, Farm nutritionist.

Information on British vegan children will be found in F. R. Ellis and P. Mumford, "The nutritional status of vegan children," *Br J Nutr* (in press), and Sanders, 1977, op. cit. The remarks by Dr. F. R. Ellis are from a personal communication. The quotation on nitrite hazard in infant foods is from Foman, op. cit., p. 484. The *JAMA* article on the low growth rate of vegan infants appeared in 228:675, 1974. See also J. T. Dwyer et al., "Preschoolers on alternate life-style diets," *J Am Diet Assoc* 72:264, 1978.

The study of feeding of solid foods to infants, "Infantile overnutrition in the first year of life," was done by A. Shukla et al. and appears in *Brit Med J* 4:507, 1972. The reference to Dr. Holliday is from *Med World News*, September 7, 1973. The quotation from Dr. William B. Weil, Jr., is from testimony before the United States Senate Subcommittee on Health and Scientific Research, June 8, 1977. The Environmental Defense Study of breast milk in vegetarians is reported in the *New York Times*, September 20, 1977, p. 50.

The quotation by Jean Mayer is from *Nutrition in Preschool and School Age*, op. cit., p. 59. The information on calcium and difficulties in pregnancies among teenagers is from G. J. Everson, *J Am Diet Assoc* 36:17, 1960; T. R. Nelson, *J Obstet Gyn Brit Emp* 62:48, 1955; and D. Baird et al., *J Obstet Gyn Brit Emp* 61:433, 1954.

For practical advice, Dr. Benjamin Spock's *Baby and Child Care*, Revised Edition (New York: Pocket Books, 1976), is still the best of its kind. The food recommendations, although tailored for omnivores, are also useful to vegetarians. Haim Ginott's two books on child psychology, *Between Parent and Child* (New York: Avon, 1967) and *Between Parent and Teenager* (New York: Avon, 1969) may be of value in solving feeding problems.

# CHAPTER 5: HEALTHY PREGNANCY ON A VEGETARIAN DIET . . .

The principal source for this chapter, in addition to those listed under "General" sources, is *Maternal Nutrition and the Course of Pregnancy* (Washington: National Academy of Sciences, 1970). The study of the fourteen pregnant vegans is in J. Thomas et al., "The health of vegans during pregnancy," *Proc Nutr Soc* 36:46A, 1977. Sanders's information on the fat content of breast milk is from Sanders, 1977, op. cit. Sanders's advice on B12 is from a personal communication. *The New England Journal of Medicine* article on the B12 deficient infant is by M. C. Higginbottom et al., 229:317, 1978. For practical information on breast-feeding see *The Womanly Art of Feeding*, Second Edition (Franklin Park, Ill.: LaLeche League International, 1963).

## CHAPTER 6: OLDER VEGETARIANS . . .

The principal sources for this chapter are *Textbook of Geriatric Medicine and Gerontology* by J. C. Brocklehurst (London: Churchill Livingstone, 1973); *Practical Geriatrics*, H. P. von Hahn, editor (New York: S. Karger, 1975); *Nutrition and Aging*, Myron Winick, editor (New York: John Wiley, 1976); and *The Practice of Geriatrics*, Second Edition, by John Agate (Springfield, Ill.: Charles C Thomas, 1970).

Dr. Leo Lutwak's theory on calcium nutrition is in "Continuing need for dietary calcium throughout life," *Geriatrics*, May 1974, p. 71. The work of the Leeds group is reported in J. R. Bullmore et al., "Effect of age on calcium absorption," *Lancet* 2:535, 1970. See also M. P. Anderson et al., "Long-term effect of low dietary calcium-phosphate ratio on the skeleton of *Cebrus albifrons* monkeys," *J Nutr* 197:834, 1977. Dr. F. R. Ellis's study of osteoporosis, "The incidence of osteoporosis in British vegetarians and omnivores," is in *Am J Clin Nutr* 25:555, 1972. Also see *Am J Clin Nutr* 27:769, 1974, for qualifications to original study. The quotation by Dr. Albanese is from *Nutr News* 39:5, 1976.

## CHAPTER 7: VEGETARIAN ATHLETES

The recommendations for athletes are largely based on *Nutrition for Athletes* (Washington: American Alliance for Health, Physical Education, and Recreation, 1971); Melvin H. Williams, *Nutritional Aspects of Human Physical and Athletic Performance* (Springfield, Ill.: Charles C Thomas, 1976); A. W. Taylor, editor, *The Scientific Aspects of Sports Training* (Springfield, Ill.: Charles C Thomas, 1975); Pre-Olaf Astrand and Kaare Rodahl, *Textbook of Work Physiology*, Second Edition (New York: McGraw-Hill, 1977); and D. R. Young, *Physical Performance, Fitness and Diet* (Springfield, Ill.: Charles C Thomas, 1977).

The information on the Tarahumaras is from M. Jenkinson, "The glory of the long distance runner," *Natural Hist* 81:55, 1972; R. S. Clegg, "Tarahumara Indians," *Rocky Mountain Med J* 69:57, 1972; J. Norman, "The Tarahumaras: Mexico's long distance runners," *Nat Geog* 149:702, 1976; W. E. Conner, "The serum lipids, lipoproteins, and diet in the Tarahumara Indians of Mexico," *Fed Proc* 51: II-171, 1975; D. Groom, "Cardiovascular observations on Tarahumara Indian runners—the modern Spartans," *Am Heart J* 81:304, 1971; H. Elrick et al., "Indians who ran 100 miles on 1500 calories a day," *Phys Sports Med*, February

1976, p. 38; and H. R. Casdorph, "Nutrition for endurance competition," *JAMA* 222:1062, 1972.

The two-phase carbohydrate-loading procedure and the role of sugar are discussed by David L. Costill in "Sports nutrition: the role of carbohydrates," *Nutrition News* 41:1, 1978. Criticism of the older three-phase carbohydrate-loading technique is found in G. Merkin, "Carbohydrate loading: a dangerous practice," *JAMA* 223:1511, 1973, and *Dairy Council Digest* 46:8, 1975.

## CHAPTER 8: THE PROTEIN MYTH . . .

Primary sources for this chapter are *Energy and Protein Requirements*, WHO Technical Report Series 522 (Rome: Food and Agriculture Organization of the United Nations, 1973); *Improvement of Protein Nutrition* (Washington: National Academy of Sciences, 1974); *Amino-Acid Content of Foods*, FAO Nutritional Study No. 24 (Rome: Food and Agriculture Organization of the United Nations, 1970).

The quotations from Adelle Davis are from *Let's Eat Right to Keep Fit* (New York: New American Library, 1970), pp. 38–39. Carlton Fredericks advocates a high-protein diet in *Food Facts and Fallacies* (New York: ARC Books, 1965), p. 272. The reference to Buddhist monks is from Lee, 1962, op. cit. The work by Nevin Scrimshaw and his colleagues will be found in N. S. Scrimshaw and V. R. Young, "The requirements of human nutrition," *Sci Am* 235:51, 1976; C. Garza et al., "Human protein requirements," *Am J Clin Nutr* 29:280, 1976; and R. Vauy et al., "Protein needs of elderly men," *Am J Clin Nutr* 30:619, 1977.

## CHAPTER 9: A PAIR OF UNUSUAL DIETS

George Ohsawa's approach to diet is covered in his *Zen Macrobiotics, The Philosophy of Oriental Medicine*, Volume 1 (Los Angeles: Ohsawa Foundation, 1965) and *Macrobiotics, An Invitation to Health and Happiness* (San Francisco: George Ohsawa Macrobiotic Foundation, 1971).

The dangers of macrobiotic diets are reported in P. T. Brown and J. G. Bergan, "The dietary status of practicing macrobiotics," *Ecology Food Nutr* 4:103, 1975. Similar cases are reported in G. Alexander, "Brown rice as a way of life," *New York Times Magazine*, March 12, 1972, p. 87. The small size of macrobiotic children is reported in J. T. Dwyer, "Physical measurements of vegetarian infants and pre-school children," *Am J Clin Nutr* 29:477, 1976. Information on Kokoh is reported in J. R. K. Robson et al., "Zen macrobiotic problems in infancy," *Pediatrics* 53:326, 1974, and in J. R. K. Robson et al., "Zen macrobiotic diets," *Lancet* 1:1327, 1973. Information on serum cholesterol and blood pressure among macrobiotics will be found in Sacks, 1974, and Sacks, 1975, op. cit.

Other informative articles on macrobiotics are: D. Erhard, "The new vegetarians," Parts 1 and 2, in *Nutr Today*, November/December 1973, p. 4, and January/February 1974, p. 20; P. Sherlock and E. O. Rothchild, "Scurvy produced by a Zen macrobiotic diet," *JAMA* 199:130, 1967; "Zen macrobiotic diets. Statement of the American Medical Association Council on Foods and Nutrition," *Nutr Rev* Suppl. July 1974, p. 27; P. T. Brown and J. G. Bergan, "The dietary status of the 'new' vegetarians," *J Am Diet Assoc* 67:455, 1975; and R. T. Frankle and F. K. Keussenstamm, "Food zealotry and youth," *Am J Pub Health*, 64:11, 1974.

Statements on the fruitarian position can be found in Herbert Shelton's *Health for the Millions* (Chicago: Natural Hygiene Press, 1968); O. L. M. Abramowski, M.D., *Fruitarian Diet and Physical Rejuvenation* (pamphlet published by Essence of Health, Durban, South Africa. Original apparently published prior to 1911); Hereward Carrington, *The Natural Food of Man* (Mokelumne Hill, Calif.: Health Research, 1963).

There are several books containing reliable, if scant, information on the diet of early humans and prehumans. Three of the most readable are *The Roots of Mankind* by John Napier (New York: Harper & Row, 1973); *Man the Hunter*, R. B. Lee and I. De Vore, editors (Chicago: Aldine Publishing Co., 1968); and *An Introduction to the Study of Man* by J. Z. Young (Oxford: Clarendon Press, 1971). Two very revealing articles are A. C. Leopold and R. Ardrey, "Toxic substances in plants and the food habits of early man," *Science* 176:512, 1972; and Anonymous, "Human evolution: life-styles and lineages of early hominids," *Science* 187:940, 1975.

The studies by B. J. Meyer and his colleagues are reported in two articles in the *South African Med J*: "Some physiological effects of a mainly fruit diet in man," 45:191, 1971; and "Some biochemical effects of a mainly fruit diet in man," 45:253, 1971; and in "The effect of a fruit diet on athletic performance," *Plant Foods Man* 1:233, 1975. H. Jay Dinshah's work on fruitarianism is reported in *Ahimsa*, the official publication of the American Vegan Society, under the title "Fruit for thought" in the March/April 1976, May/June 1976, November/December 1976, and January/March 1977 issues.

# CHAPTER 10: A CLOSE LOOK AT VEGETARIAN FOODS . . .

General sources for this chapter are Robert S. Harris and Harry von Loesecke, editors, *Nutritional Evaluation of Food Processing* (Westport, Conn.: Avi Publishing Co., 1960); Robert S. Harris and Endel Karmas, editors, *Nutritional Evaluation of Food Processing*, Second Edition (Westport, Conn.: Avi Publishing Co., 1975); and *Toxicants Occurring Naturally in Foods*, Second Edition (Washington: National Academy of Sciences, 1973).

The evidence for the more extreme adverse effects of phytic acid will be found in J. G. Reinhold et al., "Zinc, calcium, phosphorus, and nitrogen balance of Iranian villagers following a change from phytate-rich to phytate-poor diets," *Ecology Food Nutr* 2:157, 1973; J. G. Reinhold, "Phytate concentrations of leavened and unleavened Iranian breads," *Ecology Food Nutr* 1:187, 1972; H. A. Ronaghy et al., "A six year follow-up of Iranian patients with dwarfism, hypogonadism, and iron-deficiency anemia," *Am J Clin Nutr* 21:709, 1968; J. G. Reinhold, "High phytate content of Iranian bread: a possible cause of human zinc deficiency," *Am J Clin Nutr* 24:1204, 1971; J. A. Ford et al., "Biochemical response of late rickets and osteomalacia to a chupatty-free diet," *Br Med J* 3:447, 1972; J. P. Carter, "Growth and sexual development of adolescent Egyptian village boys," *Am J Clin Nutr* 22:59, 1969.

Ancel Keys's work on the beneficial effect of beans is described in his book *The Benevolent Bean* (New York: Noonday Press, 1967). His work has been confirmed by R. Luyken et al. in "The influence of legumes on the serum cholesterol level," *Voeding* 23:447, 1962.

The *Lancet* recommendation on aflatoxins will be found in an editorial in 2:1133, 1973. Evidence for the adverse effect of hydrogenated fat will be found in F. A. Kummerow, "Symposium: nutritional perspectives and atherosclerosis—lipids in atherosclerosis," *J Food Science* 40:12, 1975, and in L. H. Thomas, "Mortality from arteriosclerotic disease and consumption of hydrogenated oils and fats," *Br J Prev Med* 29:82, 1975. Evidence against the adverse effect of hydrogenated fat will be found in R. B. Alfin-Slater et al., "Nutritive value and safety of hydrogenated vegetable fats as evaluated by long-term feeding experiments with rats," *J Nutr* 63:241, 1957.

Arnold Ehret's theories will be found in *Mucusless Diet Healing System* (Beaumont, Calif.: Ehret Literature Publishing Co., 1953). There is an abundance of literature on fasting and longevity but see particularly: C. M. McCay "Experimental prolongation of the life span," *Bull NY Acad Sci* 32:91, 1956; A. J. Carlson and F. Hoelzel, "Apparent prolongation of the life span of rats by intermittent fasting," *J Nutr* 31:363, 1946; M. H. Ross, "Length of life and caloric intake," *Am J Clin Nutr* 25:834, 1922; and M. H. Ross and G. Bras, "Lasting influence of early caloric restriction on prevalence of neoplasms in the rat," *J Nat Cancer Inst* 47:1095, 1971. The reference to Hodgkin's disease and cancer of the uterus is from J. Solomon, "Starving cancer," *The Sciences* 11:22, 1971. The U.S. Army experiment on fasting is reported in C. F. Consolazio et al., "Metabolic aspects of acute starvation in normal humans: performance and cardiovascular evaluation," *Am J Clin Nutr* 20:684, 1967.

The 1974 French study on breast milk and organic food is from "Le lait maternel," *Nature Progress* 4:21 by C. Aubert.

# Index

Major subject headings are shown in boldface type.

# Index

# Index

# Index

# Index

in England, 25
fiber and polyunsaturated fat, 33n
health problems in earlier days, 25
inadequate, examples, 25
of Korean monks, 25
National Academy of Sciences approval, 25
riboflavin in, 35
soy milk, problems with, 31, 35
without soy milk, 35
substitutes for animal foods, 31, 127–32
variety, importance of, 30–31
vitamin B12 in, 16n, 20, 29, 31–33
vitamin D and, 34, 35
Vegan diet, adolescents. *See* Vegan diet, children, adolescents
**Vegan diet, adults, 25, 29–36**
controlling fat on, 33
coronary heart disease and, 14–16
food guide, 30
in weight loss, 36
**Vegan diet, children, adolescents, 49**
calcium, 49, 50
food guide, children, 49
growth on, 41–43
iron, adolescent females, 49
test of adequacy, 43
vitamin B12 and, 49
vitamin D and, 50
**Vegan diet, infants, 40–44**
animal protein and, 43
calcium in, 41–43
English studies, 41–42
The Farm program for, 40
iron in, 41–42
lack of official guideline for, 40
malnourishment on, 40–41, 43
nitrate hazard, 42
order of food introduction, 43
oxalic acid and, 42
protein in, 43
soy milk in, 40–41
vitamin B12, 41
vitamin D, 41–42
**Vegan diet, pregnancy, lactation, 53–56**
breast milk, composition, 54
calcium in, 54–55
nutritional supplements in, 56
protein in, 54–55
suggested servings, 55
vitamin B12 in, 54–55
Vegetarian diets
beginning on, 21–22
cancer and, 17–18
carbohydrate, proportion in, 68
coronary heart disease and, 14–17

flatulence and, 66, 93
nutritional adequacy, 135, 139
risk of vitamin, mineral deficiency, 20–21, 31–35
typical menus, 134–36
variety in, 22
**Vegetarian diets, athletes, 62–69**
carbohydrate in, 68
carbohydrate loading, 68–69
controlling bulk, 67
fruitarian, 83–84
high-energy sports, 67–69
nutritional supplements for, 69
when overweight, 66
pregame eating, 66–68
protein in, 63–64
sugar in, 67
weight loss as danger signal, 66
**Vegetarian diets, children, adolescents**
breakfast, importance of, 50
difficulty of, 46–47
feeding problems, 50–51
**Vegetarian diets, older adults, 57–61**
**Vegetarian foods, 89–102**
agar, 98
baby foods
iron-fortified cereal, 40
packaged, 38, 39, 42
soy milk, 41, 43
beans, 91, 93–95
as basic vegetarian food, 22, 29, 103–4
blood cholesterol and, 93
as calcium source, 34
at The Farm, 25
flatulence and, 66, 93
soy beans, 93, 103
uncooked, 84–85, 93
bran, 100
bread, fortified, 34–35
bread, unleavened, 91
brewer's yeast. *See* Vegetarian foods, nutritional yeast
butter, 96
carob, 100
carrageenan, 34
cereals, 91–92
infant, 40
pretzels, 99
refined, 39, 91
rice, 24, 39, 76, 79
rye, 91
saltines, 99
unrefined (whole grain), 39, 91
wheat, 91
cheese
Alemtejo, 96
cottage, 96
ricotta, 96
vitamin B12 content, 23, 96
chocolate, 51, 100
coffee, 14, 21
creamers, frozen liquid, 31

dairy products, 96, 100
eggs
as cholesterol source, 13
fertilized, 99
iron in, 20
nutritive value, 13
protein quality, 72
vitamin B12 in, 96
vitamin D in, 96
fats and oils
hydrogenated, 97–98, 130
limiting of, 23–25, 33
margarine, 24, 35, 98
oil, cold-pressed, 99
oil, refined, 99
fruit
apricots, 90
citrus, 90
dried, 90
juices, 90
peaches, 90
protein in, 73
watermelon, 90
gravy mixes, prepared, 99
honey, 100
legumes. *See* Vegetarian foods, beans
lentils. *See* Vegetarian foods, beans
milk, 96
as calcium source, 33–34, 47–48
protein quality, 72
raw vs. pasteurized, 100
miso (soybean paste), 93
nutrient content. *See* Food composition tables
nutritional yeast (brewer's yeast), 97
calcium/phosphorus ratio, 60, 97
nuts and seeds, 95–96
higher protein varieties, 84
sesame, 34
organic food, 99
peas. *See* Vegetarian foods, beans
**salt, 12**
consumption by Eskimos, 12
consumption by Japanese, 12
in foods, 98–99
hypertension and, 12
iodized, 99
sea, 99
substitutes for, 12
seaweed
kelp, 100
vitamin B12 in, 32
soups, canned, 99
soy milk
as calcium source, 34, 41–42, 54–55
how to fortify, 96–97, 128
as problem in vegan diet, 31, 35
as protein source, 41, 43, 54–55

181

# Index